Advance Praise for *The Mentor's Toolbox*

"A must-have for any mentor or student of personal development…"
—Bryan Halverson

"*The Mentor's Toolbox* is a practical and inspiring book for professional mentors and coaches, as well as parents and educators alike. Bailey provides excellent instruction with a multidimensional approach that anyone of any circumstance can use to remove blocks and achieve the success they desire in their life. The organized and simple format of this timeless and relevant literature makes for a great reference and guide book for years to come."
—Dori Woodbury

"Every chapter has so much goodness and, as promised by the title, plenty of tools to use. It is a must-have for coaches or anyone interested in personal growth!"
—April Benincosa Francom

"This information can be used by any level of mentor so they can help their clients meet their goals."
—BJ Blinston

"*The Mentor's Toolbox* delivers us exactly that: a concise yet well-equipped toolbox, showcasing a vast array of techniques described and taught in Eric Bailey's brilliant cut-to-the-chase way. A definite must-have for the aspiring and for the seasoned mentor alike!"
—Ana Ferrinho

"Eric Bailey's *The Mentor's Toolbox* is an amazing guide for anyone looking to level up in their ability to mentor and coach. He breaks down each tool in order to make them easy to apply to all of life's challenges, assisting in making us not only better mentors, but better human beings. I am looking forward to applying these methods to my own practices."

—Bridget Schulthies

"If you just bought this one book, you would be on your way to transforming lives! This book has it all."

—Esther Laiacona

The Mentor's Toolbox

101 POWERFUL AND PROVEN
TOOLS FOR REACHING
HIGHER LEVELS OF SUCCESS

ERIC BAILEY

Copyright © 2019 Eric Bailey

ALL RIGHTS RESERVED

No part of this book may be translated, used, or reproduced in any form or by any means, in whole or in part, electronic or mechanical, including photocopying, recording, taping, or by any information storage or retrieval system without express written permission from the author or the publisher, except for the use in brief quotations within critical articles and reviews.

ClientServices@FeelWellLiveWell.com
www.FeelWellLiveWell.com

Limits of Liability and Disclaimer of Warranty:
The authors and/or publisher shall not be liable for your misuse of this material. The contents are strictly for informational and educational purposes only.

Warning—Disclaimer:
The purpose of this book is to educate and entertain. The authors and/or publisher do not guarantee that anyone following these techniques, suggestions, tips, ideas, or strategies will become successful. The author and/or publisher shall have neither liability nor responsibility to anyone with respect to any loss or damage caused, or alleged to be caused, directly or indirectly by the information contained in this book. Further, readers should be aware that Internet websites listed in this work may have changed or disappeared between when this work was written and when it is read.

Printed and bound in the United States of America
ISBN: 978-0-9987865-3-7

DEDICATION

This book is dedicated to all of the amazing mentors I have had in my life, especially my wife, Heather. Without all of you and the amazing things that you have taught me, none of this would have been possible. From the bottom of my heart, thank you!

Table of Contents

Introduction 1

Chapter 1: Getting Started 5
   Goal Setting 6
   Personal Success Equation 8
   Process of Manifestation 11
   The Law of Gestation 13
   Staying Committed 15
   Sign-in Sheet 17

Chapter 2: Visualization 21
   Champion Training 23
   Vision Board 25
   Vision Board/Dream Board Map 30
   Vision Board Success Album 31
   Dream Board 33
   Who I Truly Am Poster 35
   Affirmations 38
   Aformations 39
   Manifesto 42
   Ideal Life Meditation 43
   Morter March 44
   Advanced Visualization 47
   Abundance Experience 48
   Celebration Journal 49
   Picture the People! 50
   Two Paths 51

Chapter 3: Emotional Release 55
- Journaling 57
- Write a Letter 58
- Nature Tantrum 59
- Gingerbread Man Exercise 60
- Rhythmic Breathing 63
- Pattern Interrupt 64
- The Six Stages of Depression 65

Chapter 4: Finding Answers 69
- Journal Prompts 71
- The Mirror Exercise 73
- Fifty Ways 74
- ABCs 76
- Eye Exercise 77
- Letter to Higher Power 79
- Getting Unstuck 80
- Procrastination List 82
- Creation Vacation 83
- AWDRR 84
- Silver Platter Principle 86

Chapter 5: Taking Action 89
- Action Step Tracking Log 91
- Accountability Groups 93
- Productivity Booster 94
- Burn Your Britches 98
- Blue Screen Time 101

Chapter 6: Breakthrough 103
- The Root Fear 105
- Scale of 1 to 10 106
- Fear-to-Funny Technique 107

Bigger Than Your Fears 110
　　Ten Seconds of Courage.. 111
　　Boxes 112
　　The Wall 115
　　Limiting Beliefs 117
　　Limiting Beliefs Purge 118
　　Limiting Beliefs to Positive Beliefs 119
　　Belief Breakthrough 120
　　Personal Breakthrough 125
　　Neuroassociation Change.. 127
　　Soul Wounds 130
　　Timeline Breakthrough 132

Chapter 7: Connection **137**
　　Receiving Compliments 139
　　One Thousand Reasons 140
　　I AM ENOUGH Poster.. 141
　　The Greatness I See in You 142
　　The Mirror Appreciation Exercise 143
　　Heart Tap.. 146
　　Heart Meditation... 147
　　Parts Integration... 150

Chapter 8: Relationships **153**
　　Love Languages 155
　　One Hundred Reasons 157
　　Three-Minute Eye Contact 158
　　Heart-to-Heart Hugs... 159
　　Holding... Giggle, Giggle, Giggle, Giggle................................. 160
　　Feelings vs. Emotions 161
　　Five-Point Communication 163
　　Personality Types... 165
　　Role Reversal... 170

Chapter 9: Health and Body Fat Reduction 171
- The Six Essentials 173
- The Void Principle 175
- Alkalization 176
- Green Smoothies 177
- Intermittent Fasting 179
- Tracking Calories 180
- Exercise Program 181
- Like to Dislike 182

Chapter 10: Addiction Recovery 187
- Taking Full Responsibility 189
- Separating the Addiction from the Identity 190
- Identify the Root of the Addiction 192
- Swish Pattern 195

Chapter 11: Wealth Creation 199
- Financial Thermostat 201
- Becoming Wealthy System 204
- Money Personality Types 208
- Debt vs. Loans 210
- The $50,000 Question 213
- Thirty-Day Spending Exercise 214
- Money Letters 215
- Money Tantrum 217
- Money Bonfire 218
- $100 Bill in the Wallet 219
- $100 Bill on the Mirror 220
- $1 Million Bill 221

INTRODUCTION

Are you a current or aspiring mentor or coach? Do you have a passion for helping people? Would you like to witness miracles take place every day of your life?

In the 1800s, many people set out to find their fortunes in the California Gold Rush. Unfortunately, very few actually became rich, because as hard as they tried to find gold, they didn't have the proper tools to do so. Among the few that did have the proper tools, many didn't know how to properly use them. So too, there are many people who love the mentoring/coaching industry and feel strongly pulled to be a part of it. They are passionate about helping people to become their greatest and highest selves, but they don't know where to begin because they lack the proper tools.

This book is designed to give you the tools and specific guidance on how to use each tool in your own life and with your clients so that you may become the most effective and powerful mentor possible. The vast majority of the tools have to do with how a person *thinks* and how a person *feels*. Author T. Harv Eker likens success to a fruit tree. The fruit represents the tangible results in your clients' lives. The mistake that most people make when attempting to implement change is targeting the fruit itself. If you had an apple tree in your back yard, and you wanted to replace it with an orange tree, would you remove all of the apples from the tree and simply hope that it would begin to grow oranges? Of course not, but this is precisely what most people do in their lives. If they aren't making enough money, they think that switching jobs will do the trick. If they are unhappy in their relationship, they believe that simply finding a new partner will make them happy. While such actions may make a small difference, if they haven't fixed the underlying issue, they are simply going to attract the same situation in their new circumstances. If you want to replace your apple tree with an orange tree, you need to first dig up the apple tree roots and then plant an orange tree. You must first address what is underground before you can see changes above ground. The roots of the tree in this analogy represent your *thoughts* and *feelings*. How you think and feel regarding something in your life make up your *beliefs*, which influence your *actions*, which then create your *results*. How do you help a person change their results? Start by targeting their thoughts, feelings, and beliefs.

Some of the tools in this book are original, some are not, but all are extremely powerful. Some tools will seem incredibly simple. They can be used by anyone at any age with any education level. Other tools may seem more advanced and may require some practice to fully master. You will learn tools on a variety of subjects, including wealth creation, addiction recovery, strengthening relationships, health, and much more. Just as someone building a house does not use every tool in his toolbox at all times, you are not expected to use every tool at all times with every client. Use your best judgment to determine which tools are right for each individual.

There may be some tools that seem weird and hokey if you have never been exposed to them before, and that's OK. I like to believe that things are only hokey if they don't work, and everything in this book works 100% of the time and is based on scientific fact and peer-reviewed data. I have used these tools in my own life and have witnessed incredible improvements. I have used the financial tools to go from welfare to millionaire, the health tools to release over 50 pounds, the relationship tools to go from sleeping on the couch every

Introduction

night to enjoying the most amazing marriage I could ever think possible, the addiction recovery tools to overcome powerful, detrimental addictions in my own life, the visualization tools to create a lifestyle that most people only dream about—and all of the tools to help my clients achieve similar results in their own lives. Put plainly, these tools work!

You may already have powerful tools that you currently use. You may be a well-established hypnotherapist, NLP practitioner, or psychotherapist. You may be thinking, "But I already have the tool that I use to help people. Why would I need more?"

The answer is very simple: most people would agree that if you wanted to build a house, it would be foolish to try to do so with nothing more than a hammer in your toolbox. As useful as a hammer is, many tools are needed to build a house. Thus, many tools are generally required to achieve a desired result. I prefer to equip myself with as many tools as I can because no single tool—regardless of how effective and powerful it is—will be right for everyone or every situation. We deal with a variety of people and circumstances as mentors; no two mentoring appointments are ever the same, and the type of tools will vary per appointment. Why not fill your toolbox with as many tools as possible so that you can be ready to help any client with their unique set of challenges?

There are three levels to using tools: Level 1 is becoming aware that tools exist. Level 2 is learning how to use the tools. Level 3 is actually using the tools to create results. The objective of this book is to at least get you to Level 2 and then *strongly* encourage you to get to Level 3 by implementing the mentoring tools you will find. It won't do much good to simply know about the tools if you aren't going to use them.

Because the tools in this book cover such a wide variety of topics, I must include a disclaimer that what you read in this book is not intended to replace proper legal, medical, financial, or psychological counsel. Please consult with the proper professionals before using any one of these tools on yourself or with your clients, and please encourage your clients to do the same. Make sure you obtain proper licensing in your place of residence to use these tools and serve as a mentor to others. When in doubt, contact your local government to find out what the local laws are regarding anything you may read in this book. It's also important to understand that this book does not contain information for growing a mentoring business. If you have this book, it is assumed that you have an existing clientele and/or that you hope to use the information in this book to change your own life. If you are looking for tips, tools, and strategies to grow a successful mentoring business, I invite you to consider joining our Successful Mentor program, which contains everything you need to create an extremely successful business. More than 80% of our graduates earn a six-figure income with their mentoring businesses their first full calendar year after graduating. For information about the program, simply send an email to ClientServices@FeelWellLiveWell.com with the subject heading Successful Mentor Program.

You were put here to do marvelous things. You were born to touch many lives. It is time for you to become the most powerful mentor that you can be. It is time to fill your toolbox.

CHAPTER 1
GETTING STARTED

Goal Setting

The very first thing you want to do once you have established a mentor-student relationship with your clients is set a goal to work towards during your time together. This could be a financial goal, a relationship goal, a health goal, a business goal, a spiritual goal, whatever they choose, as long as it is within the scope of your practice. Make sure that the focus of the goal is something positive rather than avoiding something that they perceive as negative. For example, the goal could be to generate an additional $15,000 over the next six months to feel greater financial peace, rather than setting a goal to pay off $15,000 worth of debt. If you are working with someone towards overcoming an addiction to sugar, rather than setting the intention to avoid sugar for thirty days, you could focus on thirty days of healthy living. Whatever the goal is, make sure that its focus is what the clients desire and not what they wish to avoid.

The goal ought to be realistic and attainable within the time frame that your mentoring program covers, but should also stretch your clients and cause them to grow. For example, if the goal is financial and your clients currently make $5,000 per month, the goal that your clients set may be to increase their income to $7,500 or $10,000 per month.

Now, your clients may say, "But I invested in your program to learn how to become a multimillionaire! I want *that* to be my goal!" Becoming a multimillionaire is certainly an excellent financial goal to reach towards, and if your clients are currently worth $1 million, increasing their net worth to $2 million, thus becoming multimillionaires, may be an appropriate goal for your mentoring program. However, if they are currently making minimum wage and expect you as their mentor to give them some magic formula that will make them an overnight millionaire, I'm afraid they will likely be disappointed. Massive success in any area takes time and requires a lot of patience and dedication. Encourage your clients to keep their end goal in mind! If they are currently making minimum wage but do want to even-

Chapter 1: Getting Started

tually become a multimillionaire, great! But remind them to not be too hard on themselves if it doesn't happen within the time frame of their mentoring program. Help your clients set realistic goals for themselves that you as their mentor can help them achieve. Again, make sure it's something that they *do* want instead of avoiding something that they *don't* want. Avoid having "debt repayment" as the goal. If this is your clients' primary focus, their brain will repeat the word "debt" over and over, which will lead to the creation of more debt. While it's good to pay off debt, focusing on creating financial abundance is a much better message to send to the brain. Celebrate all of your clients' successes and encourage them to do the same while learning from all of their setbacks. Once the program is completed, invite your clients to reevaluate where they are and what they want to achieve next. They can then decide if they would like to extend their time with you or find their next mentor. The journey to success is lifelong.

Encourage your clients to keep in mind their purpose—their "why"—for achieving their goal. This will help them stay committed and focused throughout your program. Explain that there are two things that they are in charge of when it comes to reaching their goal: the "what" and the "why," and there are two things that they are *not* in charge of: the "how" and the "when." They choose the goal that they desire to achieve (the "what") and their purpose for achieving it (the "why"). It is then up to the universe to provide the "how" (the exact details of how everything comes together for them) and the "when" (the exact timing of it coming together).

Invite your clients to answer the following questions:
The goal I choose to focus on during this mentoring program is…

My purpose, or "why," for achieving it is…

This will provide clarity in setting the intention during your time together.

Personal Success Equation

There may be times that people will hire you as a mentor without a clearly defined goal. They know they eventually want to be happy, healthy, and wealthy, but are unsure of what "vehicle" they need to get them there.

When this happens, explain to your clients that each person's path to success is unique and different. What may work for one individual may not work for another. If they wish to increase their results, they will need to find what their personal path will be. This is done by finding their Personal Success Equation. This comes from a simple formula taught by Sharon Lechter which says GS + GP = PSE, meaning Greatest Skill + Greatest Passion = Personal Success Equation.

Invite your clients to make two lists, one that includes their top five skills and one that includes their top five passions.

Top 5 Skills	Top 5 Passions
1)	1)
2)	2)
3)	3)
4)	4)
5)	5)

It's totally fine if your clients would like to include more than five, but eventually they will need to narrow it down to one item on each list that is their greatest skill and their greatest passion. Now help your clients figure out a way to put the two together to create a product or service that is easily marketable, can fill a need that others have, and add value to the lives of others. For example, when I did this exercise years ago, I realized that my greatest skill was giving B.E.S.T. treatments, and my greatest passion was teaching. I decided to create

Chapter 1: Getting Started

classes and mentoring programs where I could teach others powerful tools and principles and then use B.E.S.T. to clear away limiting beliefs that were holding them back from putting them into practice. I began to offer my classes to others for compensation, and thus the mentoring and training sides of *Feel Well, Live Well* were born, which now accounts for over 90% of our company revenue. Remember that while assisting your clients to find their personal success equation, it must be used to create something *marketable* that fills a *need*. If, for example, they decide that their greatest skill is humming and their greatest passion is watching butterflies in the forest, their personal success equation will be humming to butterflies in the forest, which isn't a very marketable service, nor does it fill a need that many people have. It is therefore unlikely to prove a sustainable vehicle to greater success. Does this make sense? If your clients need to choose a different skill or passion on their list to create a product or service that would be more marketable, invite them to do so.

Invite your clients to answer the following questions to help them find their personal success equation:

My greatest skill is…

My greatest passion is…

The product or service that I could create by combining my greatest skill and greatest passion is…

The problem that this would solve/need that this would fill is…

The type(s) of people that need this product or service is/are…

I can market this product/service by…

My personal success equation is…

Encourage your clients to keep their personal success equation in mind throughout their mentoring program. It is now time to take action. Invite your clients to research business laws and licensing requirements in their town and then get to work creating their new vehicle to success.

Chapter 1: Getting Started

Process of Manifestation

The elite class has understood the way that the brain works for thousands of years. Only within the last century has the ability to manifest absolutely anything become publicly known. It is more simple than most people understand. The process of manifestation is this: **thoughts lead to feelings, feelings lead to actions, and actions lead to results.** It is your job as a mentor to make sure your clients understand this concept.

It all begins with thoughts. Have you ever noticed that some people seem to be happy all the time? Every time you talk to them they comment on how great the weather is or how good your hair looks or how proud they are of their children. What kind of feelings do positive thoughts bring about?

On the flip side, have you ever known someone who always seemed to be negative? They always seem to have something to complain about and are usually the ones that have an "I can't" mindset. What kind of feelings do negative thoughts bring about? This is why the vast majority of the mentoring tools found in this book have to do with the mind and how a person thinks.

Our thoughts and our feelings form our *beliefs*. All of us have various beliefs; some have to do with spirituality, some have to do with money, and some have to do with the way others see us. Our beliefs dictate our actions. Think about that for a moment. A person who believes in God will be more likely to attend church than a person who does not. A person who believes himself to be a smoker will usually smoke. A person who believes that exercise is overly painful will rarely exercise. A person who believes that money is the root of all evil will likely never accept business opportunities that could amass a large fortune. A person who believes that abundance is their birthright will likely do what it takes to create abundance. Our *results* are created by our *actions,* but if your clients desire to change their results, you must first begin by helping them change their *thoughts* and *feelings.* This is why the Emotional Release and Breakthrough chapters of this book are so important—they help clients do exactly that.

Chapter 1: Getting Started

The Law of Gestation

This is one of the nine laws of conscious creation. Simply put, it states that everything has a time frame during which it must gestate before being created in the physical world. This will be a critical principle for your clients to understand; some of their goals may take longer to achieve than they originally anticipated. If they do not understand this principle, they may become frustrated and tempted to give up.

We find this law, of course, in the animal kingdom with some mammals taking longer to gestate their young in the womb than others. It is the same when it comes to goals. Each area of your clients' lives has a different gestation period. Their fitness gestation period is different from their finances gestation period. Their relationships gestation period will be different from their spiritual gestation period. Each person has different gestation periods. Encourage your clients to be patient with themselves. You would never see a mother elephant get frustrated that her baby elephant is taking 626 days longer to gestate than a baby field mouse takes to gestate. For most people just starting on their journey to financial success, it may take several years to gestate $1 million. However, once they begin to master the process of wealth creation, they may find that it takes less and less time. Bill Gates' gestation period for that same $1 million is a couple of hours. Working with mentors (like yourself) and daily champion training (page 23) can be used to shorten the gestation periods when it comes to your clients' goals.

Encourage your clients to be careful not to compare themselves to others. Others may be working on the exact same goal that they are, only to achieve it much faster simply because their gestation period in that area of their lives may be shorter than your clients' gestation period. Encourage them to be patient with themselves and to stay on the right path, knowing that they are getting closer and closer to success each day. The only competition that they need to participate in is with themselves. Invite them to be a little better today than they were yesterday, and a little closer to their goals tomorrow than they are today.

Remember the analogy of the Chinese bamboo plant. It shows zero sign of visible growth for several years after it is planted. It isn't until the fifth year after it is planted that it sprouts. What is it doing the first four years after it is planted? Simply forming and strengthening its roots. During that fifth year, once the plant finally becomes visible, it skyrockets up to ninety feet within a number of weeks. This may be the case with your clients as well.

If you have clients that don't achieve their goals during their time with you, don't worry. If they have done all that they can possibly do and they still don't seem to have any visible results, that doesn't mean that all is lost or that their program was a waste of time and money. Be patient with them. It doesn't mean that they are a failure or that you didn't know what you were doing as their mentor. It simply means that your clients have been establishing their roots and, if they continue to do the things that they have learned throughout the program, when the time is right for them, they will skyrocket.

Chapter 1: Getting Started

Staying Committed

Have you ever known a couple that celebrated their seventieth wedding anniversary and were still every bit as in love as the day they got married, if not more so? At the same time, do you know couples who separated after only a few months? What is the difference between those who maintain happy, successful marriages and those who do not? Most people would agree that the biggest difference is *commitment*.

There is an interesting trend going on, which is couples can get married with the mutual agreement that they get to "test it out" for a month, and if things aren't all that they thought it would be after one month, they mutually agree to divorce. After one month! And then it's off to their next marriage. I personally know of someone who has been married over a dozen times. At the same time, do you know of someone who gets really excited about a new business idea, jumps in with both feet, and runs with it for about a month, only to decide it "wasn't really for them" and gives up? We see this with a lot of amateur network marketers. They attend a gathering where they get really excited about a particular company, sign up, tell all their friends and family about it, only to decide that it wasn't really the company for them, so they join another one and repeat the cycle. On the flip side, have you ever watched an entrepreneur start a business and stick with it, through the good times and the not so good times, until it becomes a thriving, profitable, successful company? What is the major difference between the successful and the unsuccessful entrepreneur? Again, the word is *commitment*.

Just because your clients now know what their personal success equation is and are working with you as their mentor, it doesn't mean that their path to success is going to be all sunshine and rainbows. Times will come that will be difficult, frustrating, disappointing, and confusing.

This is normal for *any* entrepreneur, regardless of how experienced he or she is. The key to success is, once again, commitment. Successfully married couples stay together because, to them, failure is simply not an option. They don't even entertain the idea of divorce. When problems arise, they fix them. When they hit rough patches, they invest in their relationship to turn things around. Your clients will need to have this level of commitment for their personal success. Encourage them to stick with their personal success equation and see it through to the end, never allowing the temptation to quit to even cross their minds. This doesn't, of course, mean that they can't adjust things along the way. Course corrections are essential to any business in an ever-evolving market. But once your clients decide on their personal path to success, invite them to commit 100% to themselves and to all whose lives they are on the earth to change that they will stick with it.

During their first appointment with you, invite your clients to place their hands over their hearts and say, "I fully commit to my personal success equation and give my word to see it through!" Have them repeat it three times.

Chapter 1: Getting Started

Sign-in Sheet

It is important to keep track of all of your mentoring appointments and to know where and how to begin. The following is an example of a sign-in sheet for you to have your clients fill out at the beginning of each appointment.

Date___/___/___   Time___:___ am/pm
Name_____
Location_____
Cell Phone_____
On a scale of 1 to 10, how are you today?
([low] 0 1 2 3 4 5 6 7 8 9 10 [high])
What one word describes you today?
_____

What were the best things that happened to you since our last visit?
_____
_____
_____

How would you describe your relationships?
_____
_____
_____

What are your main concerns today?
_____
_____
_____

The Mentor's Toolbox

What do you want to accomplish in this session?
_____
_____
_____

List habits that are <u>not</u> working:
_____
_____
_____

List habits that are working:
_____
_____
_____

List obstacles that you faced this week, either people or circumstances.
_____
_____

Chapter 1: Getting Started

Read through their answers before officially beginning the appointment. You will know where to start because one of the answers will be slightly more indented than the others. Whenever the subconscious mind recognizes that there is emotion behind a particular statement, it will naturally leave a small space for that emotion when the statement is written. This is where you will begin, saying, "Tell me about ____" (whatever the question revolves around).

There may be times when clients leave an entire question blank. Do *not* begin there. There is so much pent-up emotion regarding this subject, whether they are consciously aware of it or not, that drawing attention to it at the very beginning of the appointment will break rapport, something that is critical for you to maintain so that your clients trust you when it comes time to assist them with breakthrough work. You may address the topic later in the appointment if appropriate, but never begin there. Always begin with the question that is most indented.

See the example on the next page. If your clients filled out the sign-in sheet as illustrated, you would begin the appointment by saying, "Tell me more about Jeff being back home." This will put you on track to finding where the breakthrough work needs to be focused.

Mentoring

Date: _____ Time: ___ am/(pm)
Name: _____
Location: _____
Cell phone: _____

On a scale of 1 to 10 how are you today?
(low) 0 1 2 3 4 5 6 7 8 (9) 10 (high)
What one word describes you today?
_____

Start here →
What were the best things that happened to you since our last visit?
Jeff is back home, started hypnotherapy, let go 6lb, made a cb, got a piano

How would you describe your relationships?
rocky

What are your main concerns today?
plateau in business, weight, $ stuff

What do you want to accomplish is this session?
clarity in future direction, help letting go of what's not mine

List habits that are not working:
Whatching Netflix when overwhelmed

List habits that are working:
champion training

List obstacles that you faced this week. Either people or circumstances.
uncertainty in family & low with high bills

- Master march to "Why do I unconditionally like myself"
- Updated vision board

CHAPTER 2
VISUALIZATION

The following tools are highly important because they stimulate the visual part of the brain. A major reason why many fail to reach their desired result is because they can't *see* themselves achieving it. The visual part of the brain is extremely powerful and is what helps stimulate ideas for action steps to be taken. Encourage your clients to use as many of the tools in this chapter as possible, especially when choosing their daily champion training.

Chapter 2: Visualization

Champion Training

The purpose of your mentoring programs is not just to help your clients achieve their goals, although this may happen, but to help them actually become better people. The better they become, the easier it will be to achieve success. I have had the privilege of working with some incredible individuals, including a multiple-time world bodybuilding champion. One of the things that he likes to say is that in order to become a champion, you must train like a champion. This is true when it comes to success. Your mind is your most important asset. You must constantly be training it to produce bigger and better results in your life, and the same is true in the lives of your clients. This is done through consistent *champion training*. Before you begin your personal appointments with your clients, invite them to select a number of activities that they will do each morning and evening to train their minds to produce success. They will keep track of what they do and how often they do it and then report back to you at the end of each week utilizing a Champion Training Tracking Log like the one on page 24. This chapter will contain a number of specific suggestions of tools and exercises that your clients can include in their daily champion training.

The Mentor's Toolbox

Champion Training

	Monday AM / PM	Tuesday AM / PM	Wednesday AM / PM	Thursday AM / PM	Friday AM / PM	Saturday AM / PM	Sunday AM / PM

	Monday AM / PM	Tuesday AM / PM	Wednesday AM / PM	Thursday AM / PM	Friday AM / PM	Saturday AM / PM	Sunday AM / PM

	Monday AM / PM	Tuesday AM / PM	Wednesday AM / PM	Thursday AM / PM	Friday AM / PM	Saturday AM / PM	Sunday AM / PM

	Monday AM / PM	Tuesday AM / PM	Wednesday AM / PM	Thursday AM / PM	Friday AM / PM	Saturday AM / PM	Sunday AM / PM

	Monday AM / PM	Tuesday AM / PM	Wednesday AM / PM	Thursday AM / PM	Friday AM / PM	Saturday AM / PM	Sunday AM / PM

Chapter 2: Visualization

Vision Board

Your clients are powerful creators, and they may not even be aware of it. Using a vision board is an effective way to train the part of your brain that is in charge of creation. You may have heard about vision boards before; you can find countless videos online of people who have created a vision board and the tools that they have used to make it more effective. While some of them may have had success, many others have not. The purpose of this section is to clarify the purpose and the "how to" of using a vision board so that you can use one to create success in your own life and then instruct your clients to use one to create results in their lives.

First of all, a vision board is a *not* a dream board. These are two very different tools. Your vision board is for your "next-level" goals, and your dream board is for your bucket list style goals. A mistake that people make is treating a vision board like a dream board. Let me give you an example.

Let's say that you are currently earning $5,000 per month. Eventually you want to become a multimillionaire that earns hundreds of thousands of dollars (or more) each month in passive income. However, this would not be your next-level goal. Being a multimillionaire and earning hundreds of thousands of dollars each month in passive income would go on your dream board. Your vision board, one more time, is for your next-level goals, which in this case may be to make $6,000 in a month.

Begin by designating a spot on the wall in your bedroom that is roughly two feet by two feet. You may do this with a poster board if you like. Divide it into nine equal sections, making three rows and three columns. Each of these sections will contain goals pertaining to different areas of your life.

Position your vision board in your room close to your bed. You want this to be one of the first things you see in the morning as you are waking up and one of the last things you see at night before you go to bed. Your brain is extremely powerful, and what you put into it as you are going into and coming out of unconsciousness tends to be what you create in your life.

Simplicity is the key. Don't try to be fancy with your vision board. The most effective vision boards are often just a number of statements on Post-it notes and simple images that have been printed off of Google Images and then taped to the wall.

Place your vision board so that the middle is just about at eye level. If your vision board is too low on your wall, it sends the message that you are "above" going for your goals, so why would your brain try? If it is too high, it sends a message to the brain that your goals are "too far out of reach."

Use the map on page 30 to put your goals in their proper places. This is important because each section corresponds with a different area in your brain.

Chapter 2: Visualization

Use a combination of images and statements. Allow some of your goals to be in the form of an image and some to be statements of whatever you desire to achieve. This is important because you have a left brain and a right brain, and you want to stimulate and train both sides.

Each goal should be short-term, meaning the perceived amount of time to achieve it should be no more than six to twelve months at the very most. It can be shorter; in fact, the main purpose of using a vision board is to shorten the amount of time that it takes to manifest good things in your life, but please make sure that you are not putting dream board or "bucket-list" type goals on your vision board.

Make sure to only have one goal in each of the nine areas of your vision board. You may choose to utilize less than all nine areas, but the brain can only focus on so many things at once when it comes to the short term.

If you are just getting started in the vision board world, make sure to put some extremely small and easy-to-achieve goals on your board. You want to begin by building up as much evidence as possible inside your mind that you are a creator, so you may consider putting some goals that you know you can achieve within a couple of minutes, hours, or days on your vision board so that you can take those items off of it to prove to your brain that you can achieve them. During the first few months that I used a vision board, I put such items as a new belt, which ended up costing me a whopping $10 that I purchased with the money I earned by picking up an extra shift at the job I was working at the time. I put a picture of an electric hand mixer on my vision board, only to be surprised with a $25 Target gift card in my inbox within a couple of weeks, which I used to order a new electric hand mixer.

Keep track of all of the goals that you achieve. Each time you achieve one of your vision board goals, pull the image or statement off of the wall, take a picture of it, and upload it to your social media page in a Vision Board Success Album (more about that on page 31). Then take a picture of you accomplishing whatever it is and upload it to that same social media page photo album. This gives your brain further evidence that you can create good things in your life. It also allows others to get behind you and support you in your goals. This also enhances your credibility as a professional mentor because it allows others to see you as an authority figure on goal achievement—which is exactly what people look for in mentors.

Each morning and evening, stand in front of your vision board. Take a few minutes to simply look at each goal and visualize having already accomplished it. Activate your feelings. The stronger you can *see* and *feel* each goal in the present moment, the faster it will come into your life.

As you focus on your goals, it is common for fears and doubts to come to your mind. You may hear voices in your head say, "You can't do that!" "That will never happen!" "You aren't able to achieve that!", etc. Keep something to write with in your hand as you look at your various goals and write these fears and doubts down on a piece of paper when they come to your mind. This will get them out of your head so they can no longer do damage. You may find that there will be times when you begin to write a single negative thought down and several more come spewing out onto the paper. Keep doing this until you feel that your "negative thought tank" is completely empty. Do this for all of your goals. Don't worry, writing these down will NOT reinforce the negative unless you specifically go back and reread the doubts that you wrote down (so don't do that!). Destroy the paper once you have finished this exercise.

Writing down the fears and doubts that come to your mind will open up space inside your mind for receiving *action steps*, or ideas that can help you get closer to achieving your goals. When these come to your mind, immediately write them down and then go and do them. The action steps may not always make sense or seem related to achieving your goal, but DO NOT discard them.

Muscle test yourself to make sure you are aligned to each of your goals. This is done by taking the index finger of your dominant hand and placing it in between your thumb and index finger of your nondominant hand, as shown in the following picture.

Chapter 2: Visualization

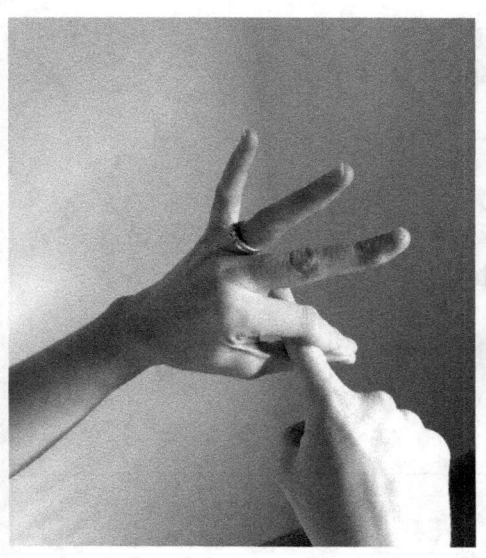 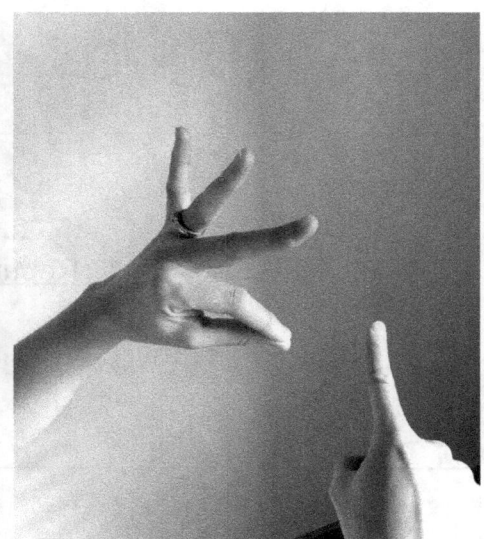

Use your dominant index finger to try to break through the barrier made by the fingers in your nondominant hand. If it holds strong while looking at each individual goal, this means that you are consciously and subconsciously aligned with that goal. If you are able to break through the barrier, this means that you are not currently aligned with that goal. If this occurs, use the Morter March tool (page 44) to realign yourself to the goal.

Note: For additional ideas and vision board strategies, please watch my YouTube video titled How to Create a Vision Board that Works, found at this web address: https://www.youtube.com/watch?v=FipEE992U1g&t=719s.

Vision Board/Dream Board Map

Wealth	Fame and/or Reputation	Spirituality
Family	Health	Love and Relationships
Learning and Education	Career and Hobbies	Travel and Fulfillment

Chapter 2: Visualization

Vision Board Success Album

This tool is used to reinforce the idea in your clients' minds that they are powerful creators. Invite your clients to create an album on their social media pages titled "My Vision Board Successes." Every time they get a goal off of their vision board, they take a picture of the image or statement that was on their wall and upload it to their social media page with the caption "Vision board image: (whatever it is)." They then take a picture of themselves achieving the goal and upload it to their social media page with the caption "Accomplished (the date)." (insert pictures)

Instruct your clients to make sure that these posts are public and not private. Doing so will serve your clients in a number of ways:

1) This method provides double evidence to your clients' minds that they are creators. The more they upload to this album, the more momentum it creates, and the more they are able to achieve. When fears and doubts surface as they go after bigger and bigger goals, they can look through this album and remind themselves how powerful they are at goal achievement.

2) Doing this exercise will help them get past their fears of being seen and judged. A major block that many people face is worrying that their peers will think negatively about them if they start to have success. Gently explain to your clients, when this happens, that it is important for successful people to put themselves out there. Some people will like them, and some people will judge them, insult them, and dislike them. It is simply part of the journey to success.

3) If your clients are aspiring mentors or coaches, this tool will help them get more clients. As you know, people hire mentors because they see them as authority figures when it comes to achievement. If people don't see your clients achieving things in their life, they are going to have a hard time attracting clients. Nearly every time

The Mentor's Toolbox

your clients post a new goal that they have achieved in this album, someone will ask how they did it. This one question is the foundation of creating a successful mentoring business.

Chapter 2: Visualization

Dream Board

What kind of a life do your clients desire to live? What does their ideal life look like? A dream board is an important tool because it allows your clients to begin to visualize how they want their lives to become. It is structured similarly to a vision board in that it follows the same nine categories illustrated in the map on page 30. While a vision board is meant for your clients' next-level goals, their dream board is for long-term, or bucket-list style goals. While your clients are only to put one goal in each section on their vision boards, they may have as many images as they would like on their dream boards. Instruct them to position the images and statements on their dream board following the same outline as their vision board. Have them place their dream board to the immediate right of their vision board on the wall. Their dream board will help give them clarity and direction. This represents their bucket list. What do they want to achieve in their life? What do they desire to experience? Their dream board will be a visual representation of this. When they look at their dream board immediately before looking at their vision board, the goals on their vision board will have more meaning. They will be the stepping stones to achieving everything on their dream board.

Encourage your clients to create their vision boards and dream boards before they officially start working with you. This will help them lay the foundation for success.

Chapter 2: Visualization

Who I Truly Am Poster

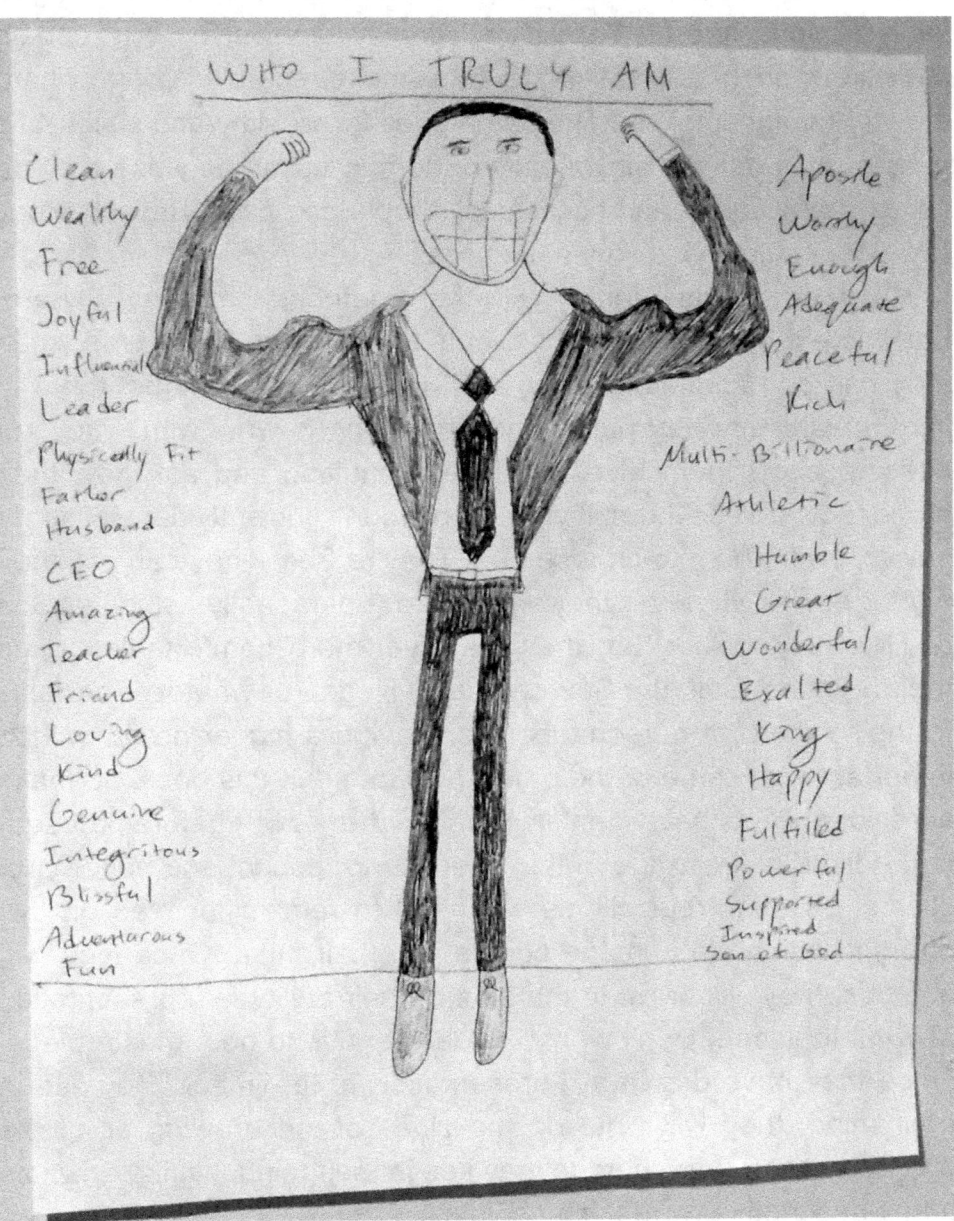

Have you ever noticed that people tend to do things according to what they identify with? For example, individuals who identify themselves with a particular religion tend to do things according to their religious beliefs. Those that identify themselves with certain addictions, such as smokers, tend to smoke regardless of how hard they try to quit smoking. The same goes for wealthy and successful people; they tend to stay wealthy and successful because they do things that wealthy and successful people do. Why? Because they *identify* with being wealthy and successful.

Help your clients identify with the greatness that they truly are. For this exercise, invite your clients to set aside some time when they can be completely alone and uninterrupted. Instruct them to take a blank sheet of paper and something to write with. They will need to allow themselves to access intuition and ask how their higher power sees them. If your clients don't currently have a higher power, invite them to choose one. They're free! They can call their higher power whatever they would like (I personally call mine God or Heavenly Father, but they may feel more comfortable calling theirs Highest Self, the Source, the Universe, or whatever pertains to their culture or personal beliefs. Having a higher power will be important with some of the other tools found in this book, so make sure your clients have identified their higher power before proceeding. Adjust the verbiage of this exercise to respect and honor your clients' beliefs). Your clients will need to remain focused on this thought until a clear image comes into their mind. Once they can see this, they will draw, to the best of their ability, a representation of what they see. Don't worry, it doesn't have to be a masterpiece. Once they have drawn a representation of the image they see in their mind, they will write on the sides of the drawing all of the characteristics of the person they see in their mind, writing down as many descriptive words as possible.

Chapter 2: Visualization

If this is how their higher power sees them, then this is who they truly are. This may be a very humbling experience. It was for me. Once your clients have completed this exercise, encourage them to place their Who I Truly Am Poster to the right of their dream board on their wall. As part of their champion training each day, encourage them to stand in front of their poster with their hand over their heart and declare, "This is who I truly am! I am...," and declare out loud each of the characteristics they have written. Again, the purpose of this is to help your clients identify with their greatest and highest self. Because, deep down, they already are this person, and as long as they stay on this path to success, there is no way that they can fail.

Affirmations

Affirmations have been recommended by law of attraction experts and mentors for years and can be defined as "positive statements that you repeat to yourself out loud to help create a desired outcome." The consistent repetition of positive affirmations can help your clients reshape their beliefs and assumptions about themselves and the world around them. This will give them a more positive perception of who they are and where they stand. They can be used for all sorts of goals, from self-confidence to relationships, wealth, and health.

An effective affirmation starts with the words "I am..." and focuses on a positive feeling created by a particular outcome. It is stated in the present tense rather than the future tense. Examples may include:

I am happy and thankful that I now enjoy my ideal weight and physique.

I am happy and thankful that I now enjoy a loving and vibrantly passionate marriage.

I am happy and thankful that I now collect and deposit $10,000 every month.

Research shows that affirmations can help you perform better under pressure, especially when stated with great passion and intensity. This can be particularly useful just before situations such as first dates and job interviews.

For best results, use affirmations in conjunction with afformations, which are explained in the next section. With both affirmations and afformations, encourage your clients to state each out loud with their hand over their heart in various tones, speeds, and intensities.

Chapter 2: Visualization

Afformations

My Declarations / Afformations

I am amazing!
Why am I amazing?

I am a clean, wealthy, physically fit family man.
Why am I a clean, wealthy, physically fit family man?

I am successful in <u>ALL</u> areas of my life
Why am I successful in <u>ALL</u> areas of my life?

I have a beautiful, fit, athletic, muscular body
Why do I have a beautiful, fit, athletic, muscular body?

I am a multi-millionaire
Why am I a multi-millionaire?

I collect and deposit hundreds of thousands of dollars in passive income every month.
Why do I collect and deposit hundreds of thousands of dollars in passive income every month?

I have thousands of people at each of my paid seminars.
Why do I have thousands of people at each of my paid seminars?

I am happy, joyful, and blissful.
Why am I happy, joyful, and blissful?

I serve here with honor and return home w/ my entire family to receive exaltation.
Why do I serve here with honor and return home w/ my entire family to receive exaltation?

There is a huge difference between affirmations and afformations, a term created by Noah St. John. As explained, affirmations can be very powerful, especially when they are done with great intensity and repetition. The only problem is, according to experts, it takes approximately 10,000 times for a traditional affirmation to actually sink in, get past the reticular activating system, and begin to take shape inside the subconscious mind.

Have you ever had a rough day where everything seemed to go wrong? Have you ever tried repeating the phrase, "Today is a wonderful day! Today is a wonderful day! Today is a wonderful day!" Even with the repetition of this phrase, does that automatically make you feel better and turn your rotten day into a wonderful day? Probably not, unless you repeat the phrase 10,000 times.

Thankfully, there is a shortcut. Putting your affirmations into "why" questions causes your brain to go to work looking for the answer. For example, if you ask yourself, "Why is today a wonderful day?" Your subconscious goes to work looking for reasons why today is a wonderful day. If you are constantly asking yourself, "Why am I collecting and depositing $10,000 in certified funds every month?" pretty soon you will likely find yourself collecting and depositing $10,000 in certified funds every month.

Invite your clients to use this tool each day, but to use great caution because it can also work against them. For example, if you ask yourself, "Why do I always feel horrible?" your brain is going to go to work looking for why you always feel horrible. Use this tool only in the positive.

Invite your clients to make a list of afformations and affirmations, put it on the wall to the left of their vision board, and recite them out loud each morning and evening as part of their daily champion training. Doing so will help balance their energy. Regardless of their gender, everyone has both masculine and feminine energy within them.. Different energies are used in different circumstances. Afformations will open up the reticular

Chapter 2: Visualization

activating system and place the mind and body into feminine, nurturing energy. Following with affirmations will then drive the point home, place the mind and body into masculine energy, and prepare your clients for taking the action necessary to manifest the results into reality.

Manifesto

A manifesto is like a life's mission statement. It details in writing the exact life that you desire to live. It creates clarity, direction, and motivation.

Invite your clients to consider all areas of their life, including the five Fs of Success (Faith, Family, Fitness, Finances, and Fulfillment). Have them write in detail what they desire each area to be like, stating everything in the present tense as if everything was happening in the present. Invite them to use their dream board as a reference if necessary. What kind of house do they live in? What kind of car do they drive? What kind of relationships do they have? What does their body look and feel like? What kind of impact are they making in the lives of others? How much money do they collect each month? How is their relationship with their Higher Power? The more details, the better. This may take several minutes, and that's OK. Their manifesto is the written equivalent to their dream board and should match it accordingly. Their manifesto, together with their affirmations and afformations, will aid in creating the next tool: an Ideal Life Meditation.

Chapter 2: Visualization

Ideal Life Meditation

If you want to create lightning fast change in your clients' lives, this tool is for you! Encourage your clients to find a recording of relaxing meditation music that they can play in the background as they create their Ideal Life Meditation Recording. With the music in the background, invite your clients to record themselves reading their manifesto, followed by their list of afformations and affirmations, concluding the recording with any words of encouragement they wish to include. This recording is their Ideal Life Meditation. Encourage your clients to listen to it each night as they fall asleep and each morning as they are first waking up. Because it will be a recording in their own voice, their subconscious will instantly accept it as truth. Remember, once the mind believes it, it can achieve it. Invite your clients to use this every day as part of their champion training.

The Mentor's Toolbox

Morter March

This tool, named after Dr. M. T. Morter, Jr. who developed the Bio-Energetic Synchronization Technique (B.E.S.T., more of which can be found at this website: https://www.feelwelllivewell.com/b-e-s-t/), is used to reset the nervous system and retrain the brain. It uses contralateral movement and stretching to put the body into such an awkward position that it causes a pattern interrupt inside the brain.

Begin the exercise by doing a simple muscle test (as shown on page 29). Place the tips of your thumb and index fingers together on your non-dominant hand—meaning if you are right-handed, you would place the tips of your thumb and index finger together on your left hand. Then place your right index finger through the hole you have just created with your left hand. Go ahead and try this right now. If you are left-handed, do the opposite. You are now going to have a contest between your two hands. With your right index finger, you are going to try to break through the two fingers on your left hand, and your fingers on your left hand are going to try to hold strong and keep your right pointer finger from breaking through. This may take some practice, but it will not be too hard after some time. Once you get it down, your left hand will usually win against your right finger, unless you think or say a negative thought. Go ahead and try the following: place your finger in the hole again and say, "Give me a yes," and try to break through your two left fingers. If you do this correctly, it should hold strong and your finger should not be able to break through. Then say, "Give me a no," and repeat the process. This time your right finger should be able to break through your two left fingers. This is how you do a muscle test and how you can find out if your subconscious is on board with your conscious desires. If it is, you can think about or look at an image of one of your goals, do this test, and it will stay strong. If it isn't, your two left fingers will be weaker, and you will be able to break through

Chapter 2: Visualization

with your right finger. That's the goal that you need to focus on when you do this next part of the exercise.

Encourage your clients to go through the items on their vision board and do this muscle test until they find a goal that causes them to go weak. Now proceed with the next part of the Morter March, which is a special stretch that will put you in a position that you're not normally in. Doing this causes the mind to say, "Whoa, time out here! We weren't meant to be in this position! What is going on?" Distracting this part of the brain allows the subconscious to locate and remove roadblocks that are keeping it from accomplishing whatever the goal happens to be.

Demonstrate this exercise to your clients by putting your left foot forward and bending your left knee just enough so that you can no longer see your foot. Your right leg goes back and remains straight, with your feet parallel to each other. Now extend your right arm up in front of you at a forty-five-degree angle, and extend your fingers wide so that your right thumb is pointing up. Your left arm will go back at a forty-five-degree angle as if you were making a straight line from your right hand to your left hand, with your fingers extended and your left thumb pointing down. Now tilt your head slightly

toward your extended right hand, close your left eye, look up at your extended hand with your open right eye, and hold your breath for ten seconds, closing both of your eyes for the final two seconds. Now breathe out and change to the other side. You will now put your right foot forward, bending the knee. Raise your left arm in front of you, extend your fingers, thumb pointing up, and put your right arm back, fingers extended with your thumb pointing down. Tilt your head slightly toward your left arm, close your right eye, and hold your breath for ten seconds, closing both eyes for the final two. Repeat this process three times on each side. You will look and feel so silly doing this the first time, but I promise there is a science behind it. If you still have trouble doing this after reading these instructions several times, simply look up the Morter March online.

Once your clients feel confident performing this exercise, they can add afformations in their mind. Putting yourself in this weird position instantly creates an opening in your R.A.S. (reticular activating system, a.k.a. your brain's filter), allowing it to feed positive ideas directly into your subconscious. If clients are focusing on a particular goal—for example, having a vibrantly healthy body—they should ask themselves, "Why do I have a vibrantly healthy body?" while performing this stretch. Instruct your clients to ask themselves the question twice with one eye open, then one more time with both eyes closed. Then take another breath, switch sides and do it again until they have done it three times on each side, having repeated the question, "Why do I have a vibrantly healthy body?" or whatever it is they are focusing on, a total of eighteen times.

Now I know what you must be thinking, and that's, "Oh my goodness, is that ever hokey!" Well, the way I look at it is that I'd rather be really hokey and really successful than really cool and really unsuccessful.. How about you? I love what one of my mentors used to say: "It's only hokey if it doesn't work," and the Morter March works every time. Encourage your clients to make the Morter March a part of their daily champion training.

Chapter 2: Visualization

Advanced Visualization

One of the fastest ways to create new beliefs is to see yourself in vivid detail already accomplishing it. One of the most effective ways to do this is to find videos online of whatever you would like to create and then watch them over and over again, imagining that you are wherever you are watching. For example, let's say you are wanting to create a trip to a certain theme park. You could go online and find videos of people enjoying the rides at that theme park. As you watch these videos, different parts of your brain are stimulated to create the feeling of actually being there. Once your brain *believes* that it can achieve it, it will.

What are your clients wanting to create in their lives? If they desire to create a trip to a certain vacation spot, encourage them to find a video of someone at that vacation spot and watch it frequently. If they desire to create having a particular car, invite them to find a video of someone driving that car. If they want a new house, help them find videos of someone doing a video tour of the kind of house they want. Together, create a playlist of videos that help them feel like they have already achieved the things they desire, and have them watch it regularly.

Abundance Experience

If you have clients that are really struggling to see themselves enjoying financial abundance, invite them to plan an abundance experience. This ought to be an experience that your clients have always wanted to have but never allowed themselves to do so because of the cost. This experience may include going to a five-star restaurant. It may include staying at an amazing resort for an evening or spending a few hours at the most luxurious spa in town. It may include a trip to an exotic location. The purpose of this tool is for your clients to give themselves permission to enjoy the finer things in life, thus allowing themselves to create greater abundance.

An old adage says, "practice makes perfect." This is incorrect, because unless you practice something perfectly, you will only ever continue to repeat the action imperfectly. A more accurate phrase says that "practice makes *permanent*." An abundance experience allows your clients to practice *feeling* wealthy so that they eventually *become* wealthy. What happens inside the brain is the building of *neuroassociations* (more about this on page 127). Everything in life is connected to one of two things inside the mind: pain or pleasure. A reason why many fail to reach success is because they link the process of becoming successful with pain. The purpose of this tool is to begin to link success with high amounts of pleasure and to make abundance a reality by experiencing it firsthand.

Chapter 2: Visualization

Celebration Journal

Celebration is the highest form of gratitude. Whatever we give thanks for by celebrating, we tend to get more of. The same is true for accomplishments. The more we celebrate our accomplishments, the more we tend to accomplish.

Invite your clients to keep a journal next to their bed, and each night as part of their evening champion training, write down the date and at least one to two accomplishments from that day. They can be huge accomplishments like earning their first million dollars, or they can be tiny accomplishments like tying their own shoes. An accomplishment is an accomplishment to the subconscious mind. This helps their brain accumulate evidence that they are a creator. This tool also serves as a pick-me-up if they are having a rough day and feeling down on themselves. If clients contact you to let you know they are feeling discouraged, you can encourage them to open their celebration journal, begin reading the accomplishments that they have achieved, and suddenly, they will start to feel better.

If, for whatever reason, it doesn't serve your clients to keep a physical journal next to their bed, they may also do this electronically by sending themselves an email each evening with the subject heading "Celebration." When they wish to go through it and read their accomplishments, all they need to do is simply go into their sent mailbox and type in the search box "Celebration." Their list of accomplishments will then come up electronically for them to enjoy.

Picture the People!

There may come times when you will work with people who are struggling with motivation or a sense of urgency to follow through with their goals and/or the action steps that they have set for themselves. If this is the case, invite your clients to close their eyes and imagine all of the people that they are here to help, serve, and influence for good in ways that only they can. Ask them to nod their head when they can see them. Next, invite your clients to tap into intuition and ask for a specific number of people that they are here to help. Once they state the number out loud, ask, "What happens if you don't help them?" After they answer, ask, "How urgent is it for you to help them?" Following their answer, ask, "What must you do in order to help all of those people?" They will usually respond with something to the effect of, "I've got to get busy!" or "I've got to get my action steps done!" Encourage your clients to keep these people in mind as they complete their action steps.

Chapter 2: Visualization

Two Paths

If you feel the Picture the People! tool would be inappropriate for your clients, or if you feel that a stronger motivational tool is needed, consider using this guided meditation exercise. The following is a script that you can use to help your clients understand the consequences of continuing to do exactly what they have been doing (making no changes) and what the consequences would be if they chose to get busy and apply what you have been teaching them. The example provided is specifically for helping someone overcome addictive behavior. Simply adjust it to fit whatever your clients need.

Start by inviting your clients to take several deep breaths in through their nose and out their mouth, closing their eyes, and clearing their mind. Continue on by reading this out loud, adapting for your clients' current circumstances:

Today you are standing at a fork in the road of your life. You have come to a decision point. Should you continue to do what you have been doing with regard to your behavior?

You think about all the problems and concerns that this behavior brings into your life.

The road on the left is a slow downward road. It is easy to take the Low Road. You could just coast down it. It is the path of doing what you have been doing for so long—but it is a path of misery. The road on the right goes upward. It will take some effort to take the High Road—but it is the way of freedom, health, and life. It is the road of being in control of your life. It is the High Road to Success!

Look at the road on the left; it means carrying all of the problems associated with continuing this behavior with you even longer than you already have. Think of how negatively this behavior makes you feel. Really allow yourself to feel the weight of the burden of this self-destructive behavior. Feel your desire to be free from all of the ill effects of hurting yourself this way.

I'm going to count from one to three, and we are going to go down that low road of being out of control one more year. 1, 2, 3! There you are, after one more year of being out of control—of being miserable because you have continued this behavior. You feel the weight of the disappointment in yourself. You notice the things that litter this painful way of living. (If it seems appropriate to the issue, point out the people associated with the problem, the negative influences.) There is a mirror there, and you see yourself and ask yourself, "Am I pleased with myself? Am I happy to have another year of this behavior? Do I feel better having made this decision? Do I feel healthier or worse? Do I look and feel better about myself, or not? Do I feel smarter?" Feel the disappointment you have in yourself for continuing with this behavior for another year.

I'm going to count from one to three and we are going to go down to the five-year point on this road of continuing with this behavior. 1, 2, 3! There you are after five more years of being on the low road. Reflect on all of the effects of that choice! Really allow yourself to feel the effects of that decision. You feel hopeless. Now look around you and see everything associated with that poor choice. Those are the things that have done this to you. So, you can't stand them anymore. If there are people associated with this behavior, are they really your friends? Do they really care about you? Again, ask yourself, "Am I pleased with myself for participating in this behavior for five more years? Do I have the right to do this to myself? Am I healthier for making this choice? How is it affecting my life? Is my life better or worse? Do I feel smarter for continuing for an additional five years?"

And now I count from one to three and we move down to the ten-year point on this low road of continuing this self-destructive behavior. 1, 2, 3! There you are after ten more years of hurting yourself by continu-

Chapter 2: Visualization

ing this behavior. Once again, reflect on all of the cumulative effects of that choice! Really allow yourself to feel the effects of that decision, of continuing for ten more years. You feel awful. You feel more hopeless. Again, you look around you and you see everything associated with that behavior. Those are the things that have done this to you. You can't stand them anymore. Maybe you even detest the sight of them. If there are people associated with this behavior, are they really your friends? Do they really care about you? How do you feel about them? There is a mirror there and you look at yourself. You ask yourself, "Am I pleased with myself for continuing for ten more years? Is my life better or worse? Do I feel intelligent for continuing for an additional ten years?" Really feel the consequences of remaining on this low but easy road.

As I count back from five to one, you come all the way back to the beginning of the fork in the road—5, 4, 3, 2, 1. You feel better now because none of that has happened yet and it doesn't have to... You have decided not to let that happen to you. You have decided to take the High Road of Success on the right! You know that it will take a little more effort, but now you know in your heart and mind that it is worth it. You have decided to start taking better care of yourself! In fact, you have already left the old way by coming here today! You are already taking your first steps toward freedom and success on the road on the right.

Let's see how this new decision to break free for life affects you. You think about all the good positive changes that becoming free from the self-destructive habit brought into your life! Being free from all those problems—the feeling of really being in control and confident. You are now on the path on the right, which means success and a feeling of energy and optimism.

I'm going to count from one to three, and we are going to go down that road of having made this change for one year. 1, 2, 3! There you are after one year of being in control. You feel great! You have done it, you are a success, you have never felt better, and you are going to feel even better yet! There is a mirror there, and you ask yourself, "Am I pleased with myself? Am I happy to have accomplished my goal for a whole year? (If it seems appropriate to the problem, point out the things/items and people associated with this new way of living and being.) Do I feel better having made this healthy decision? Do I feel smarter?" Feel the pride and health that is inside of you. Was it worth it? Do you want to continue to stay on the High Road of Success?

I'm going to count from one to three and we are going to go down to the five-year point on this road of being successful in making this change! 1,2,3! There you are after five more years of success, of reaping the rewards of making this permanent change. Five years of being in control and energized! Now reflect on all of the effects of that choice! Really allow yourself to feel the effects of that decision. You feel strong. Everything in your life is better for having made this permanent change. Enjoy the feeling of knowing that you have made a permanent change, knowing that you will never go back to the old way.

And now I count from one to three, and we move down to the ten-year point on this High Road of Success. 1, 2, 3, and there you are after ten more years of making this good and positive change in your life. Bring forth all of the effects of that smart choice! Really allow yourself to feel the effects of that decision, of continuing to be in control for ten more years. The old behavior is now simply something that you used to do. It was a mistake to have ever done it, but now you are free and will remain free for the rest of your life! You look in the mirror one more time and ask yourself, "Am I pleased with myself for being completely free for ten more years? Would I ever go back to that old bad habit of hurting myself? Am I glad that I have made this permanent change? A change made for good?" Of course you are!

As you end this visualization, ask your clients, "With this newfound motivation, what are your next steps to take?"

CHAPTER 3
EMOTIONAL RELEASE

Have you ever thought about a dream that you had and really started to feel good about it . . . right until the moment when doubts and fears started coming into your mind, and you ended up feeling even worse than you did before because you suddenly felt hopeless because there was no way that the dream could ever come true? One of the amazing things about the visualization tools is that they cause doubts, fears, and negative emotions that are stored inside you to come to the surface. Once they come to the surface, you can clear them out. Why is this important? It's because again, absolutely everything in our lives is linked to one of two things inside our minds: pain or pleasure. Human beings are naturally pain avoiders and pleasure seekers, and so if there is something in our lives that we believe will bring us pain, whether it's true or not, we will tend to avoid it. Let me give you an example. Have you ever met someone who really wanted to release weight and get fit? They were extremely overweight and not happy with their body, but they never attempted to slim down, or if they did, they very quickly gave up and reverted back to their old habits because, deep down inside, they believed that the process of releasing weight and getting fit would be painful? They believed that they would have to give up the foods that they love and start that "crazy" process called exercise that they try to avoid at all costs! Just thinking about exercise and dieting gives them anxiety! Until they release the negative emotions surrounding diet and exercise, they will continue to associate the process of releasing weight with pain and won't ever do it. Again, this is why the visualization tools are so important because they usually cause any negative emotions, fears, or doubts to come to the surface. For example, you may look at your vision board and see the goal that says, "Collect and deposit $10,000 per month." If, as you do, you feel super excited and confident, great! You're on the right track! But if you start looking at the $10,000-a-month image and feel anxious, hopeless, fear, or doubt, that's when the tools in this chapter will be extremely valuable, both for you personally and with the people you mentor.

Chapter 3: Emotional Release

Journaling

Simply writing down your negative thoughts, feelings, and impressions can be extremely powerful. Wait, write them down? Won't that reinforce the negative thoughts? Only if you go back and reread them over and over again. The simple act of writing something down is a way to transfer the energy from that negative thought, feeling or doubt from your brain onto paper. Remember, *emotion* is simply *energy in motion*. Removing the energy from an emotion makes it so it can longer negatively affect you. Share this with your clients.

As your clients use visualization tools, doubts will likely come to their mind, such as, "You can't do that!" "That will be too hard!" "You'll never get that!" Instruct your clients to write these negative thoughts down when this happens and then destroy the paper. This sends a message to the brain that they are in control, not their fears or doubts.

This can also work if they ever feel overly stressed about something. Your clients may be amazed at how much of a difference it makes to take a quick moment to journal on whatever it is that is stressing them.

Write a Letter

As a mentor, you already know the importance of relationships and how damaging holding onto anger, hatred, and resentment towards another person can be. If you have clients that are struggling in their relationships, and you can tell that they need to let off some steam so that healing can take place, this may be the tool that you turn to. It is simple: invite your clients to write a letter to the person towards whom they feel anger, hatred, resentment, or any other negative emotion. Inform your clients that they will not actually be sending the letter. This is simply a way to move the emotion from inside your clients down onto paper.

Chapter 3: Emotional Release

Nature Tantrum

How long does a young child hold a grudge? Most of the time, not very long. What do they do if someone upsets them? They throw a tantrum, release all of their anger, and then continue playing as if nothing had ever happened.

What would your life be like if you were able to release negative emotion as quickly as children?

There may be circumstances when clients have so much pent-up emotion within them that simply journaling or writing a letter isn't enough to release it. What can you do? Send your clients to a place where they can be totally alone to throw a tantrum. They will likely give you a look as if to say, "Wait a second, I can't do that! I'm a grown-up! Grown-ups don't throw tantrums!"

A mistake that many adults make is thinking that they have to hold their emotions in. Many of us were told not to cry as kids. Were you told this as a child? Perhaps you got in trouble if you cried or threw a tantrum, which created a limiting belief that carried over into your adult life, making it difficult for you to release pent-up emotion. My invitation to you is to allow yourself to throw a tantrum every now and again, and give your clients the same invitation. Obviously, make sure no one is around who can hear or disturb you, so go somewhere where you can be totally alone and express yourself completely. Allow yourself to feel and release all that needs to be felt and released.

I tell people that if you're having a crummy day, allow yourself to recognize and validate the fact that you're having a crummy day. Tony Robbins counsels, "See things as they truly are but not worse than they are." Once you've acknowledged that you're going through a rough time, throw your tantrum, get the emotion out of you, and then pick yourself up and move on.

The Mentor's Toolbox

Gingerbread Man Exercise

Chapter 3: Emotional Release

This is an extremely intense exercise that combines several emotional release tools and is used when you can tell your clients have deeply rooted resentment, anger, or other negative emotions regarding an individual or group of people. Invite your clients to take a piece of paper and draw a rough outline of a human being. I am definitely not an artist, so whenever I do this exercise it usually ends up looking like a really lopsided gingerbread man, hence the name of the exercise. Have them draw a face and some hair and then label their "gingerbread man" at the top with the name of the person toward whom they harbor negative emotions. This will serve as a visual representation of that person. Next, ask your clients to stand and prop up the drawing somewhere where they can easily see it, like on their chair or a desk. Then invite them to call the person's name out loud and ask for permission to fully express what has been on their mind. For example, if your clients feel resentment towards someone named Mary, they would draw a representation of Mary, stand up, and then say *out loud*, "Mary, may I express myself to you?" Have them wait until they hear a "yes" in their mind. Once they have, invite them to proceed to verbally express absolutely anything and everything that needs to be expressed to that person, holding nothing back, completely letting go, and continuing to speak until they feel that their emotional tank is completely empty. If they need to yell, encourage them to yell. If they need to scream, encourage them to scream. But remember, this must be done *out loud*. If they try to do this only in their mind, the negative emotion will actually get lodged even deeper inside their bodies. Expressing themselves out loud allows the energy to be released.

Once they feel that they have verbally expressed everything they need to express, invite them to experience a *physical* release of emotion by destroying the paper. If they feel like they need to punch the paper, let them punch it. If they want to rip its head off, let them rip its head off, or stomp on it, or tear it to shreds, or burn it—whatever it takes to allow a physical release of negative emotion to take place. Once this is complete, invite your clients to pick up the pieces of paper and prop them back up on the chair or wherever it was before. Warn them that this next step may be the most difficult part of the exercise, because in order for full healing to take place, they must now ask for forgiveness for holding onto those negative emotions. They might put up a fuss, saying, "But that person did this and this and this to me! Why should I ask for forgiveness from them?" Gently remind your clients that they were the ones who held onto the negative emotions, and the words "Will you forgive me?" must leave their lips for this tool to be effective. Invite them to look at what's left of the paper representation of the person and ask for forgiveness for holding onto the negative emotions towards them.

Finally, invite your clients to imagine that the person's greatest and highest self is standing in front of them, having heard everything that has been expressed, and then, speaking out loud as if they were that person's greatest and highest self, invite your clients to say the words that they imagine that person's greatest and highest self would say to them. These may be words of apology, an expression of love, a deeper understanding; whatever it is, this is what completes the healing process. Again, invite your clients to imagine that the person's greatest and highest self is now standing in front of them, and speaking as if they were that person's greatest and highest self, what message would they speak? Once they have completed this step, invite them to say, "I forgive you, and thank you for serving me," and then have them imagine themselves embracing that person.

Chapter 3: Emotional Release

Rhythmic Breathing

This is an emotional shielding exercise that I use during moments of high intensity during my mentoring appointments. If, for example, I am assisting a client with a gingerbread man exercise, I need to make sure that I do not absorb any of the negative emotion that is being released. Rhythmic breathing achieves exactly that.

Start by breathing in for the count of four, then hold your breath in for the count of four, breathe out for the count of four, hold it out for the count of four, and repeat the process. Try it right now: breathe in ... 2 ... 3 ... 4, hold it in, 2, 3, 4, breathe out, 2, 3, 4, hold it out, 2, 3, 4, breathe in ... hold, breathe out ... hold, and continue. Doing this exercise actually activates a part of your nervous system which makes it so that negative emotional energy cannot affect you. It also helps you to release stress and become present in the moment. Use this tool during moments of high-intensity emotional release during your mentoring appointments, and invite your clients to use it any time they feel stressed.

The Mentor's Toolbox

Pattern Interrupt

Have you ever been in the middle of a deep conversation with someone when something out of the ordinary happened that momentarily distracted your train of thought, and when you tried to continue the conversation you could no longer remember what you were talking about? Perhaps this happened when you noticed another person with whom you needed to chat walk by, or when a child interrupted you to tell you they needed to use the bathroom. This is called a pattern interrupt and can be a powerful tool to use with your clients that you can tell have negative emotions surrounding a particular person or circumstance that need to be released.

Invite your clients to talk about the problem they are facing in their life in great detail, really emphasizing the negatives of the situation. For example, if your clients have negative emotions regarding money, invite them to describe in great detail an experience that they had that gave them evidence that money caused pain. Invite them to really allow themselves to feel the negative emotions that they felt during the experience. As they begin to talk about the experience, watch their countenance. About ten seconds into their story, suddenly do something to cause them to lose their train of thought. You might startle them. You might shout, "Stop! Stand up and twirl around ten times and then sit back down!" You might even throw a little bit of water in their face. This momentarily stops neurons in your clients' brains from firing, thus helping to release the negative emotion. You'll know that you have done this effectively when you ask your clients to continue talking about the experience that they were sharing, and they won't be able to because they can't remember how it felt. This may take a few times, meaning you may need to have them start and stop their story with you interrupting them several times before they finally get to a point where they will no longer be able to feel the pain of what they were saying. Continue this exercise until your clients can discuss the problem without feeling any sort of negative emotion.

Chapter 3: Emotional Release

The Six Stages of Depression

Every day, millions of people around the world experience major bouts of depression. As a mentor, you will likely work with people who struggle with very real mental illness. The information in this section is designed to help you identify and recognize the six stages of depression so that, accompanied by competent medical and psychological help, you can help your clients survive and overcome the symptoms they may be facing.

Depression comes in six main stages. Each stage comes with its own unique set of challenges and action steps. The action steps utilized by an individual in one stage of depression will usually be inappropriate for someone else in another stage.

The first stage is the deepest stage of depression. All motivation is lost during this stage. Survival is the only thing on a person's mind who is in this stage. In extreme cases, those in this stage may experience suicidal thoughts because they feel hopeless. Because of this, there is no desire to do anything that would bring any amount of happiness or help overcome the depression. It doesn't help that others say things like, "Just snap out of it." Telling a person in the first stage of depression to "just snap out of it" can actually cause them to sink even deeper into depression because shame for feeling the way that they feel is added to the feeling of depression.

The action step during this stage is simply honoring and validating the feelings of depression. There is no need to feel guilty or shameful for being depressed. This is where a lot of mentors and coaches get stuck because, again, people hire us to help them overcome their challenges, so when we have our own challenges, it can be really scary at times and downright depressing because we then feel like we have no right to help others through their problems when we don't have everything figured out in our own lives.

If you have clients in stage one of depression, invite them to honor and validate their feelings by planting both feet firmly on the ground, shoulder width apart, and shouting, "I feel depressed, and it sucks!" Give your clients permission to feel the way they do. They may find that the cloud of depression begins to dissipate once its existence is acknowledged.

If you study chakras, a person in this stage will usually have a blocked root chakra. Planting the feet and validating the feelings of depression helps to unblock this chakra.

The second stage is where you "want to want" to feel better. Does that make sense? You aren't ready for actively trying to feel better, but you do wish that you could feel better as long as you can do something *passive*. If you have clients that are in the second stage of depression, invite them to watch a funny video or listen to uplifting music to at least get their head above water and start smiling. A person in stage two will usually have a blocked sacral chakra, and doing something passive will help them to feel nurtured, which helps unblock this chakra.

The third stage is when you want to feel better; you are tired of feeling depressed and are ready for a change. As it may be difficult to find something in the present to be happy about at this stage, invite your clients to choose something in the future that they can look forward to—it could be a vacation, a special occasion, or something they could create. Doing this can spark a wave of creativity that can help pull your clients out of depression.

A person in stage three will usually have blocked solar plexus and heart chakras. The action steps described in this section help to unblock these chakras.

The fourth stage is when a person is ready to reach out for help and begin to feel better. If you have clients who are in this stage, explain to them that it is critical that they do not try to overcome this stage on their

Chapter 3: Emotional Release

own. Invite them to reach out to loved ones who can help boost their spirits, as well as seek professional help. Encourage your clients to use their intuition to seek the help that would be right for them, be it with medical professionals, psychiatric professionals, B.E.S.T. practitioners, mentors, Timeline Breakthrough practitioners, hypnotherapists, or whatever is right for them. They must use their voice to ask for help and explain what is going on in their life. Doing so will help to unblock the throat chakra, which is usually blocked in stage four of depression.

If you or someone that you love needs additional resources, send an email to ClientServices@FeelWellLiveWell.com and let our team know that you or a loved one is suffering from depression and would like some additional help. We can get you in touch with licensed professionals who can help, usually at no charge.

The fifth stage takes place after getting outside help, and is when you get *moving*. Physical activity, especially in fresh air, invigorates the mind and releases endorphins in the body. Find an exercise program that works for you, even if it's simply going for a five-minute walk out in nature. Exercise and time spent in nature helps open the third eye chakra, which is typically blocked in stage five of depression.

The sixth stage is when you are finally ready to *look for lessons* that can be learned from the events that triggered the depression. As you know, every experience in our lives is designed and calculated to teach us certain lessons. Pain without learning equals suffering, but pain *with* learning leads to breakthrough. If you have clients in stage six, ask them what positive lessons they can learn and retain from the experiences they have gone through. Invite them to write these lessons down and to feel gratitude for the experiences they have had. Depression can be dispelled with pure gratitude. The Timeline Breakthrough tool found on page 132 may be appropriate to facilitate this stage and help your clients finish overcoming depression once and for all. The crown chakra is the typical block at this stage; to unblock it, feel and experience sincere gratitude in life.

The Mentor's Toolbox

CHAPTER 4
FINDING ANSWERS

The Mentor's Toolbox

The tools in this chapter have to do with helping your clients find answers. There will likely come a time when your clients ask you a question that you don't currently have an answer to. This is 100% OK by the way . . . Just because you are their mentor doesn't mean you have to know *everything.* What you do get to do is guide your clients to finding their *own* answers, which, again, is what the tools in this category are all about.

Chapter 4: Finding Answers

Journal Prompts

This tool is very similar to the first tool in the emotional release chapter, and that is giving your clients a journal prompt and inviting them to write down the first answer that comes to their mind. Putting pen to paper is like unlocking the gates of the subconscious mind. As a mentor, you know that the subconscious mind holds the answers to all things, and that it's simply a matter of accessing it to receive those answers. At times, it will be your job as the mentor to help your clients do so.

For example, I recently met with one of my private mentoring clients who was having a hard time overcoming a particularly personal trial. This client of mine had been battling resentment toward certain men in her life, and she was, unconsciously, pushing money away. This was showing up in the amount of money, or lack thereof, she was making in her business, and was also affecting her personal life. (A little bonus tidbit of information: people—women especially—store three things inside the same file in their subconscious minds: men, God, and money. Typically, if someone has had a negative experience with one, to one degree or another, they will push away the other two.)

I invited her to write out a number of prompts, leaving space in between each one for answers, including:

The reason(s) for me going through this trial . . .
The lesson(s) I am to learn include . . .
This will ultimately serve me and be to my benefit because . . .

I invited her to write down the very first thing that came to her mind after reading each prompt. The first things that come to a person's mind will often seem to not make sense; answers directly from the subconscious mind are rarely logical, but that doesn't make them any less true. My client ended up writing down amazing answers which finally gave her the perspective that she was looking for and helped her to realize that men weren't her enemy, that the trial she was going through was actually very much a blessing in disguise, and that she no longer needed to push money or her husband away from her. Can you guess what happened? Up until this point, she had been struggling for months to attract even a single new client into her business. I received a text from her later that evening informing me that, within three hours of our mentoring appointment and her breakthrough, she closed a $30,000 client. Thirty thousand dollars within three hours of having her breakthrough—all because she wrote down a series of journal prompts and allowed herself to put pen to paper, writing down whatever came up to mind. Journal prompts are one of the most effective tools in helping clients find answers.

Chapter 4: Finding Answers

The Mirror Exercise

Invite your clients to close their eyes and take a few deep breaths in, exhaling through their mouths, to clear their mind and become totally present. Then invite them to see in their minds a full-length mirror and view their greatest and highest self, the one who has all experience, all knowledge, all wisdom, and can answer any and all questions regarding their greatest and highest good. Invite your clients to nod their head when they can see that in their mind. Then invite them to pose whatever questions they may have out loud as well as say the first answers that come to their minds. For example, if they are struggling to find their next step towards achieving a particular goal, invite them to ask, "Highest self, what is my next step?" and then speak whatever comes to their minds first. Different people will do better with this exercise, and others will prefer the written journal prompts. Both tools are used to find answers, so find out which tool works best for each individual client.

Fifty Ways

This is used to help a person find a way to achieve a seemingly impossible goal. Just as the name implies, it includes inviting your clients to make a list of fifty different ways that they could possibly go about achieving the goal. For example, years ago when I needed to come up with $100,000 in seven days, I grabbed something to write with and simply began making a list of anything and everything that came to my mind regarding how I could generate $100,000 in seven days, which I had never done at that time. Of course, several of the first answers were ridiculous things, such as rob a bank, sell a kidney, create an abstract painting and claim that it's an original Pollock and sell it on eBay—absolutely ridiculous things that I would never actually do. What this did, however, was open my mind to possibilities and allow the creative juices in my mind to flow. Pretty soon, after I had written between ten to twenty ridiculous answers, I began to think of some ways that would actually work. Seven days later, I had manifested the $100,000 that I needed. Again, this is a tool that you can use with clients who don't know how they are going to reach a certain goal.

Invite your clients to number a piece of paper from one to fifty (or to 100 if you want to be extra ambitious) and write down any idea that comes to them, regardless of how crazy it may seem. Remind them that writing an idea down doesn't mean they need to do it; they are simply writing down possibilities for now. Real ideas will start to come once they have written a certain number of ridiculous ideas down. Once they have all fifty ideas written down, invite your clients to cross off any that aren't legal, moral, and ethical, and then start narrowing their list down to the top ten or twenty. Once they do, invite them to put their ideas in the chronological order they feel is best to take action on

Chapter 4: Finding Answers

those ideas, and then commit to getting them done by a specific date and time. They now have a clearly laid-out plan for how to achieve their goal, and it all came from their own mind. You were simply the facilitator. This tool shows the power of possibility thinking.

ABCs

Invite your clients to divide a piece of paper into three columns and label them A, B, and C respectively. The C column is for what they see themselves accomplishing, meaning what their current goals are. Perhaps they write down "earn $100,000 this year; publish a book; run a marathon." This is the column that they fill out first. Next, invite them to fill out column A, which is where they are currently at in each of the areas that they wrote down in column C. Maybe they say they are currently on track to making $50,000 this year, have written the first chapter of their book, and can currently run no more than one and a half miles at a time. The B column represents what they need to do in order to achieve everything in column C. Maybe they write down that they need to make five more prospecting calls per day to generate more business and more income, take a writing course to improve their writing skills, and learn how to properly train their bodies to work up to run a marathon. Column B helps them figure out what they are missing. Finally, invite your clients to think of people that they need to talk to in order to get the additional help that they need to achieve each one of their goals. Explain that a goal is just one person away. Invite your clients to follow the advice they receive from the people they spoke to as well as what they wrote down in column B. They now have a clear path to take to reach their goals.

Chapter 4: Finding Answers

Eye Exercise

You have likely heard that the eyes are the windows to the soul. They are also windows to finding answers.

Have you ever asked a person how to do something that was seemingly impossible? I will sometimes do this with a volunteer at my seminars. I will choose a member of the audience who hasn't created $25,000 in a single month and ask them how they will generate $25,000 in the next seven days. What usually happens is the audience member will think about the question for a moment and then respond, "I don't know." If the rest of the audience is paying attention, they will usually catch what happens.

Whenever a person is posed a question that they have never pondered before, their eyes will usually wander. Sometimes they will glance up, sometimes they will glance to the right. Other times they might look down for a second and then look up and to the left. The client's subconscious mind is looking for the answer to the question.

Imagine that the mind is a library with a book on every subject imaginable and an answer to any question they could ever imagine. The eyes are the mind's librarians. When a person is asked a question to which they do not consciously have an answer, their "librarians" will go directly to the part (or parts) of the mind's library where the book containing the answer is found. What happens most of the time is the client will subconsciously find the answer, reject it because it seems illogical, or the question is too difficult or scary, and then come back to conscious awareness, causing them to respond with, "I don't know."

As a mentor, you know better! You know that the subconscious mind holds all answers and has access to all knowledge. It is your job to help them find those answers and then take action on them.

Explain to your clients that you are going to pose a question to which they may not currently have an answer, and that finding the answer will be key to knowing how to best move forward. Tell them that, once you pose the question, you are going to give them three minutes to silently ponder the question and allow their eyes to wander freely and naturally, wherever they want to move. During the three minutes, chart where their eyes go. If they go up and to the right, take note of that. If they go down, take note of that as well. Once the three minutes have passed, go through your clients' eye movements with them. Show them where their eyes went, and then invite them to hold their eyes in each of the positions, one at a time, while posing the question to themselves over and over again until at least one answer comes to their mind. Once answers come to them, invite them to write them down. Then have them ask themselves if there are any more answers that need to come from that eye position. If their intuition tells them "yes," invite them to keep their eyes in the same position and continue to pose the question to themselves until they feel that all answers from that "book" have been revealed. Repeat the process with all eye positions that you documented. Once they have all of their answers written down (these will often be action steps, or things that they need to do in order to achieve a certain goal), invite your clients to put their action steps in the order they feel they need to accomplish them. They now have a clear set of instructions on how to achieve their seemingly impossible goal.

Chapter 4: Finding Answers

Letter to Higher Power

If you ever have clients that seem to have a disconnect between them and their higher power, invite them to write a letter to their higher power to express their concerns about their life. Encourage them to write down whatever comes to them, and no, this is not sacrilegious in any way as you're simply helping to release toxic, negative emotions from inside your clients. Once they have written their letter, invite your clients to write a response letter as if they were their higher power, writing anything and everything that comes to mind, disregarding if it makes sense or not. This may help them gain perspective regarding different areas of their lives. You can use this tool for anyone, not just one's higher power—for example, you could write a letter to your mother-in-law expressing whatever it is you want to express. Now, keep in mind that you aren't actually going to send this letter to them; this is just a way for you to release negative emotion and experience a breakthrough. Once your clients have finished writing their letter, take a quick break and then invite them to write a return letter, starting with "Dear (whatever your client's name is)." Instruct your clients to write down whatever comes to mind. They may be shocked at what they end up writing. This will usually help your clients find more clarity and closure when it comes to what they perceived as negative experiences in their life.

Getting Unstuck

There will come a time when you work with clients that feel stuck, not entirely knowing what they desire to work on or how to go about working on it. What is typically happening internally is they aren't feeling completely fulfilled. A lack of fulfillment, however your clients define it, can leave a person feeling down, unmotivated, and even depressed.

When clients express feeling stuck, first invite them to identify their primary love language (more about love languages on page 155). Next, invite your clients to put the following words in the order of importance according to them: love, joy, happiness, peace, security, fulfillment, acceptance, respect, admiration.

The one that they deemed as the most important is usually the one that they aren't receiving enough of. Invite your clients to rate on a scale of 1 to 10 how much they feel they receive of their primary love language and the feeling they felt was most important from each of the following:
- Self
- Higher Power
- Family
- Other people

For example, if their primary love language is loving touch, and they felt that respect was the most important of the feelings, you would invite your clients to rate the following:

On a scale of 1 to 10, I believe that I receive loving touch from the following:
- Self
- Higher Power
- Family
- Other people

Chapter 4: Finding Answers

On a scale of 1 to 10, I believe that I receive respect from the following:
- Self
- Higher Power
- Family
- Other people

Once this is completed, invite your clients to set specific action steps to improve any of the areas that are rated less than a perfect 10. Completing these action steps will help your clients feel better, get unstuck, and increase performance levels.

Procrastination List

Do your clients ever express that they feel overwhelmed with things that need to get done and important decisions that need to be made? Do they say that it feels like their brain isn't working properly to get started?

Sometimes simply making a procrastination list frees up enough space in your brain to allow you to focus. Sometimes, writing things down and then allowing yourself some time to take a break and recharge does the trick, allowing your brain the time it needs to work out solutions to the challenges you are facing. A lot of people find that writing down a question or challenge that needs an answer or solution just before going to sleep and allowing their subconscious to work on it throughout the night works best. They often wake up with answers and exciting new ideas.

So if you ever feel "stuck" or that your brain is on overload, try the following three things:

1) Write things down/make a to-do list

2) Give yourself a break and allow your brain time to "turn itself back on"

3) Write down a question just before you go to bed and allow your subconscious to find the answer

Chapter 4: Finding Answers

Creation Vacation

If your clients still feel stuck after utilizing the other tools in this chapter, invite them to consider taking a "creation vacation." This is a chance to get away, allow themselves to be in an abundant atmosphere, and allow their brain to create ideas naturally. Some of my most lucrative ideas have come from creation vacations that I have taken with my wife.

Here are some guidelines for creation vacations:

1) Make sure to go with people who support what you do and who can contribute ideas. This can include business partners, company executives, mentors, spouses, whoever you feel would best contribute to the creation of ideas. I do *not* recommend taking children on creation vacations.
2) Invest in food, lodging, and activities that promote a feeling of abundance. Just like an abundance experience (page 48), the more successful you feel during this vacation, the more successful ideas you will be able to create. This is *not* the time to be cheap.
3) Take a notebook or another way to capture ideas as they come to you. Even if the ideas don't seem to make sense, make sure to immediately write them down.
4) Allow ideas to flow naturally. Don't try to force them. When you put yourself in a state of creation, creation will come.

If your clients have been working diligently to achieve their goals but still seem stuck, invite them to take a creation vacation as soon as possible.

AWDRR

This is a tool that I strongly encourage you to teach your clients. AWDRR is an acronym for Ask, Write, Do, Report, Receive the Reward. Your clients may not know what action steps to take if they have never achieved a certain goal before. And unless you are a personal trainer that literally lays out workouts for your clients to do each and every day, it won't be up to you to tell them what their action steps will be. This will come as they learn to tap into their intuition and trust what they receive. "Ask" means asking their intuition what they need to do that day to get just a little bit closer to their goal. If your clients are spiritual or believe in the power of prayer, you can encourage them to ask their higher power first thing in the morning what their action step ought to be. Invite them to clear their minds and to really listen and then write down whatever comes to mind. Ask, write, next comes do. They then *do* whatever their action step— or action steps in some cases—happens to be before they go to bed that night. Once they've done so, they then get to report in their action step tracking log (example on page 91) that they completed their action step. This creates a feeling of accomplishment inside the brain, and again if they believe in the power of prayer, invite them to report back to their higher power that night that they did what they were impressed to do. They then get to receive the reward. This reward may be something as simple as a warm feeling of accomplishment or receiving the next piece of the puzzle, meaning further inspiration for action to be taken. It may be that the very next day they receive a very tangible reward for their efforts. For example, there have been several times when my action step for the day was to post something on my social media account, and when I did, my reward was an impression to reach out to certain people who had commented, which then led them to attend one of my classes and be so impressed with what I do that they signed up for private mentoring with me and paid me tens of thousands of dollars. Imagine if I received an impression to post something and waved it off because it didn't seem to make sense. Had I done so, I never would have received those rewards. If you have clients that seem to have a hard time doing this exercise and receiving answers regarding inspired action steps, it is likely that there have been times in their life where they have felt impressed to take certain actions but ignored the promptings. I have found that inspiration tends to only go to those who follow it, and if we set a precedent of not following through when we receive inspiration, eventually that inspiration stops coming to us.

Silver Platter Principle

Whenever you work with clients that struggle to receive inspiration, it is usually due to one of three reasons:

1) **They don't write down ideas when they come to them.** I like to imagine that there is an inspiration department in the sky that is extremely generous when it comes to ideas, but only if the recipients are excellent *stewards*. Have you ever woken up in the middle of the night with an excellent idea but failed to write it down before going back to sleep? What happened? You likely forgot it by the time you got out of the bed the following morning. Encourage your clients to write their ideas down *immediately* once they receive them. I personally like to use my phone's email app for this. Anytime I receive an idea, I email it to myself with the subject heading being whatever it pertains to. For example, whenever I received an idea related to this book, I emailed it to myself with the subject heading "The Mentor's Toolbox Book." That way all of my ideas stayed organized. When I needed to pull them up, I simply clicked on the "Sent Mail" button and typed "The Mentor's Toolbox." Encourage your clients to do the same.

2) **They don't actually follow through with the ideas they are given.** An easy way to stop receiving ideas and inspiration is to not put them into practice. If your clients have been struggling to receive ideas, ask them how often they do what they feel impressed to do. If you notice a pattern of not following through, it will be your job as a mentor to strongly encourage that this change.

3) **Their platter is too full.** Some people simply have so much information and so many ideas in their head that there is no room to receive more. Imagine that the mind is like a silver platter and

that ideas and inspiration are like manna from heaven. A platter, regardless of how large it is, will eventually become full and unable to hold any more manna if it is never emptied. Promptly writing ideas down, doing them, checking items off of procrastination lists, and creation vacations are all effective ways to "empty the platter," thereby creating room for new ideas.

The Mentor's Toolbox

CHAPTER 5
TAKING ACTION

The Mentor's Toolbox

One of the most important parts of any mentoring program is the action that is taken towards creating change. Change cannot happen if a client does not take action. The tools in this chapter are designed to facilitate this.

Chapter 5: Taking Action

Action Step Tracking Log

Name_____

Goal_____

	Date	Action Step	Completed Yes / No	Excuse
Monday				
Tuesday				
Wednesday				
Thursday				
Friday				
Monday				
Tuesday				
Wednesday				
Thursday				
Friday				
Monday				
Tuesday				
Wednesday				
Thursday				
Friday				
Monday				
Tuesday				
Wednesday				
Thursday				
Friday				
Monday				
Tuesday				
Wednesday				
Thursday				
Friday				

The Mentor's Toolbox

An effective way to monitor your clients' progress is by having them fill out an action step log. Invite your clients to write down a specific action step that they will take each day, utilizing the AWDRR principle (page 84), to get them a little closer to achieving their goal. They write down their action step in the morning and then check whether or not they completed it in the evening. Encourage them to take a picture of their tracking log and send it to you each Friday. As you look it over each week, look for patterns. Are your clients taking inspired action each and every day that you can see will bring them their desired outcome? Are they simply filling their time with "busy work" (action steps that keep them busy but will not actually bring them closer to achieving their goal)? Are they slacking off on certain days of the week? Be the other set of eyes that your clients need to fix their blind spots.

Chapter 5: Taking Action

Accountability Groups

A great way for your clients to have daily accountability without having to report directly to you is to form accountability groups. I like to hold bonus trainings for my top-level clients where I invite them to my home for dinner, give them some exclusive training, and then invite them to form accountability groups with three or four other people in the program. Once your clients have formed their groups, let them know that they will be reporting to this group every weekday for the next three months. Invite them to set a time each day that they will commit to a brief conference call where they take turns stating their names, the goal that they are working towards, their action step for that day, and then whether or not they did it. If done correctly, this call should only take five to ten minutes maximum. This helps people to let go of their excuses, because no one wants to have to report that they didn't keep their commitment. Each member of the group holds the others accountable and will give encouragement as well as gently, kindly, but firmly call each other out when needed. This allows you to delegate the job of daily accountability to your clients. You can still invite them to send you daily text messages with their progress, but this gives them a group of positive peers to help them move forward. Please note that I do *not* encourage clients to have daily calls when only one man and one woman are getting on the call without the rest of their group. They must always have at least three people on the call.

The Mentor's Toolbox

Productivity Booster

A mistake that many new entrepreneurs make is thinking that they have to fill their time with busy work, even when that work isn't actually bringing in new clients. Instruct them that what they ought to focus on is *productivity* more than simply being *busy.* The following guidelines can help your clients get significantly more done in less time.

1. **Always get a full eight hours of sleep**. A common misconception among new entrepreneurs is that they have to train their bodies to survive on only a few hours of sleep so that they can spend more hours working. Studies have proven time after time that this simply doesn't work. Many medical studies have shown that those that consistently get six hours of sleep or less actually have the same cognitive performance as that of someone who is drunk. Most people would agree that it would be pretty silly to attempt to do much work while drunk, but many entrepreneurs do exactly that when they consistently get too little sleep. Invite your clients to make getting the rest that they need a priority. For some people, this means getting to bed by 9 p.m. and waking up at 5 a.m. every day. For others, this may mean going to bed at 2 a.m. and sleeping until 10 a.m. during the day. While there are some mentors that swear that anyone who wants to be successful must be awake before dawn, I am a firm believer that the important thing is finding what works for you and what works for your clients. Some of the most successful people that I know are night owls who get their best work done in the late hours of the night while everyone else is sleeping, and then sleep in until late morning or even early afternoon. As long as your clients are putting in the effort, consistently doing their action steps, making progress, and seeing results,

Chapter 5: Taking Action

don't worry too much about when they get their eight hours of sleep, just that they *get* eight hours of sleep.
2. **No checking emails, text messages, voicemails, or social media for at least one hour after waking up**. This may take some getting used to, because most people are in the habit of reaching for their phone first thing in the morning upon waking up. The main problem with this is whatever we put into our minds first thing in the morning sets up our whole day. One negative message can throw off one's energy and productivity for the whole day if read within the first hour of waking. The first hour after waking should be used exclusively for the following:
    a. Prayer/meditation/connecting with the Divine
    b. Gratitude work
    c. Visualization/champion training
    d. Listening to uplifting music, inspirational talks, books, or quotes
    e. Stretching/yoga/exercise
    f. Goal setting
    g. Positive self-talk
3. **Set certain times during the day when you *do* respond to your messages, and keep this commitment religiously**. Unless you are some sort of on-call emergency technician, turn off *all* notifications on your cell phone. Yes, *all* of them, including text messages, email, social media, phone calls, and keep your phone on *do not disturb* except during specific times during the day that you designate exclusively for responding to messages. I suggest setting aside one hour in the morning and one hour in the afternoon. Your employees and clients will get used to you not responding until those times of the day. They most likely aren't going to die if you

don't get back to them immediately. The problem that many people face is literally being controlled by the notifications on their phones. They get used to checking their messages way too frequently and getting sucked in to responding to every little notification that comes their way. This drastically decreases productivity. Encourage your clients to set an hour in the morning and an hour in the afternoon exclusively for responding to their messages and then not look at their phones for the rest of the day unless they absolutely have to. If they find that this amount of time is insufficient, they can make adjustments, but only after committing to this principle for as long as you feel is necessary to break the habit of always checking their cell phones.

4. **Work for one hour at a time and then take a ten-minute break**. Studies have shown that the most productive intervals of time for work are between fifty to ninety minutes. Get tasks done for an hour without interruption (following the third guideline will greatly help facilitate this), take a break, go for a quick walk in nature to reset your mind, and repeat the process.

5. **Schedule one hour of personal "me time" (a.k.a. blue screen time) each day**. This time is used exclusively for doing whatever recharges you. This could be spent working on a hobby, reading a book, going for a walk, working out, or whatever helps you feel fulfilled and allows you to unwind for the day.

6. **No electronics during the last hour before you go to bed.** The only exception is if you use some sort of meditation recording to fall asleep. Avoid watching television, surfing the internet, or responding to messages right before you go to bed. Electronics reduce sleep quality and thus decrease

Chapter 5: Taking Action

productivity levels. Read a book instead, or write in a journal, meditate, pray, and allow your mind to unwind from a full day of productivity.

Encourage your clients to follow these guidelines for maximum productivity.

The Mentor's Toolbox

Burn Your Britches

There are a lot of people that aren't willing to do what it takes to reach the desired outcome that they have set for their lives. You may have clients that fall into this category. They may have attended some seminars, maybe they've started a business, maybe they've paid you a large sum of money to teach them certain skills and help lead them to success. Unfortunately, there have been times when your clients aren't willing to actually take the necessary steps toward reaching success.

A lot of mentors teach the concept of "burning their bridges behind them." What exactly does it actually mean to burn one's bridges? Let's say that your clients are trying to get to a magical watering hole (let's call it the fountain of youth), and in order to get there they have to cross a number of challenging obstacles, including a rickety old bridge, to get to the other side of the mountain where the fountain of youth is found. Your clients cross this bridge only to find that there are still a number of obstacles in front of them. They will still have to stretch themselves and get outside their comfort zones in order to reach the fountain of youth where they have always dreamed of going. The idea of burning one's bridges behind them means that, once the bridge is crossed, they destroy the bridge so that there is no way that they can turn back before reaching the fountain of youth. So your clients get out their lighters, set the rickety old bridge on fire and watch it burn. They have literally burned their bridge behind them, making it impossible for them to take a "chicken exit," turn around and head home. Again, this is the concept that many within the mentoring industry teach. Unfortunately, there's still one problem. Even though your clients have eliminated their chicken exits and made it so that they can no

Chapter 5: Taking Action

longer go back, nothing is keeping them from simply sitting down right where they are, crossing their arms and legs and thinking, "I'm not going any farther! I'm staying right here! I am done!"

The sad reality is some clients do this, even while participating in high-level mentoring programs. There are many who think that, just because they hired a mentor, everything in their life is going to change without them actually doing anything. Any time new opportunities are presented to grow and learn more, they still turn them down because of some excuse that they have. They might say, "Oh well, I've already invested all that I possibly could in this one mentoring program, so I don't have the money to do any more," or, "Well, I'm already spending a lot of time with this other mentor, so I don't have the time to pursue other opportunities." They don't really change much in their lives because they haven't jumped in to the pursuit of success with both feet; then they wonder why they are not getting results.

Some even start blaming you as the mentor, saying things like, "What a waste of money this program was!" They start a downward cycle of putting too much energy into what they *don't* want, so naturally they start expanding everything in their life that they don't want.

Instead of encouraging your clients to burn their bridges, I invite you to encourage them to burn their *britches.* Think about that for a moment. Let's say that your clients have crossed the bridge and are now on the side of the mountain where the fountain of youth is. Let's say that your clients have a magical lighter that creates a magical fire that can only be put out by the water in the fountain of youth. Let's say that your clients then light their britches on fire. If they did, and the only way that they could actually put out the fire was by getting to the fountain of youth, of course they would do it! Who cares what type of obstacles they encounter or what type of challenges they need to overcome along the way! They would do it because they don't want to burn their bum off completely, which would happen if they failed to reach their destination!

The biggest difference between the successful and the mediocre is that successful people are willing to (figuratively) burn their britches. Studies show that very few people are self-motivators, only about 10% of the world's population. What that means is that about 80% of people—or the vast majority—need some form of outside motivation to achieve their goals. This might come from a mentor or an accountability partner. On the far end of the spectrum, there are some people that have to have certain areas of their life hit rock bottom in order for them to change. Encourage your clients to light that fire underneath them and get to where they want to go.

Chapter 5: Taking Action

Blue Screen Time

As important as exercise, smart work, and productivity are, it is also important to take time to rest. A lot of people follow the "all work and no play" mantra. They are the extreme go-getters, and they work hard each and every day because, to them, there simply isn't time for anything else. We see this especially with full-time mothers. They are so selfless, and they love their families so much that they never create time just for themselves.

Encourage your clients to allow themselves some time each and every day just to pamper themselves, to rest and recuperate. Think about that for a moment. If you were trying to strengthen your muscles, what would you do? You would probably regularly put time in at the gym and lift weights. People that work their muscles know that it is unproductive to lift weights using the same muscle group every single day until they pass out from exhaustion. They know that they need to do a certain number of repetitions, then rest, then a certain number of repetitions, and then rest, and then give their bodies a number of days to rest completely so that their muscles can heal and rebuild themselves even stronger. The same concept applies when it comes to resting your *mind*.

If your clients want their brain to continue to grow stronger and produce more results in their life, they must give it downtime, or what I like to call *Blue Screen Time*. You know how a computer screen will turn blue when it is recharging and updating itself? It's the same idea.

Each person is different; everyone has a different method that helps them to relax and recharge. For example, my wife takes care of our little kids each day as a stay-at-home mom, but each night after she puts our kids to bed, she takes a nice warm bath to recharge, relax, and let her mind calm down. That's her way of getting Blue

Screen Time. Personally, I like to watch fun videos on the internet or read a good book in order to recharge my own batteries.

Find out what your clients enjoy doing to relax, recharge, and rejuvenate their minds. Encourage them to set time aside each day (preferably an hour) exclusively for relaxing and unwinding. If they resist, claiming that they simply "don't have time to do so," remind them that everyone has the same amount of time: twenty-four hours each day. Everyone has time for things they prioritize. Encourage your clients to make Blue Screen Time a priority and allow their productivity levels to skyrocket.

CHAPTER 6
BREAKTHROUGH

As a professional mentor, you understand that fear is one of the most debilitating emotions that a person can experience. The definition of fear is the anticipation of discomfort. Many clients will struggle to really go after a goal because they believe that the process of achieving it will be highly uncomfortable. If they perceive the process of change as more uncomfortable than staying stagnant, change isn't going to happen.

Our beliefs create our reality—the more limiting beliefs a person has, the smaller they are going to play the game of life. The tools in this chapter are designed to help overcome fears and turn limiting beliefs into empowering ones.

Chapter 6: Breakthrough

The Root Fear

Often, the fears that we feel are really just surface distractors that deter us from what we really fear underneath. The way to find the actual underlying root fear is by asking your clients to share what their biggest fear is. Let's say that they respond that their biggest fear is failure. Ask them, "What would be the worst part about failure?" They may then respond that failure would mean that they had disappointed their parents. Ask them, "What would be the worst part about disappointing your parents?" Continue to do this until your clients draw a blank and can't think of anything else. This may take a few minutes, and occasionally the clients may go in circles. Be patient with your clients during this process and keep at it until they draw that blank or say, "That's it." You have now found the underlying root fear and can proceed to help your student overcome it using another tool in this category.

Scale of 1 to 10

Most fears come from the emotional side of the brain. A simple, yet highly effective tool for removing the energetic charge of fear is inviting your clients, anytime they begin to feel a certain fear, to ask themselves how strongly they feel the fear on a scale of 1 to 10. The act of measuring their fear puts them back into the logical side of their brain where fear doesn't exist.

Chapter 6: Breakthrough

Fear-to-Funny Technique

I had a very vivid nightmare when I was six years old that kept me up at night for years. In the nightmare, I was observing a group of young children playing near the edge of a tall, jagged cliff. They kept getting closer and closer to the edge which, if they fell off, would lead to their imminent death. I kept wanting to shout at the children to not get any closer because something bad was going to happen if they did, but they couldn't hear me. For years, I would close my eyes to sleep at night, and the image of the cliff would come into my mind, bringing with it all of the emotional fear that accompanied it.

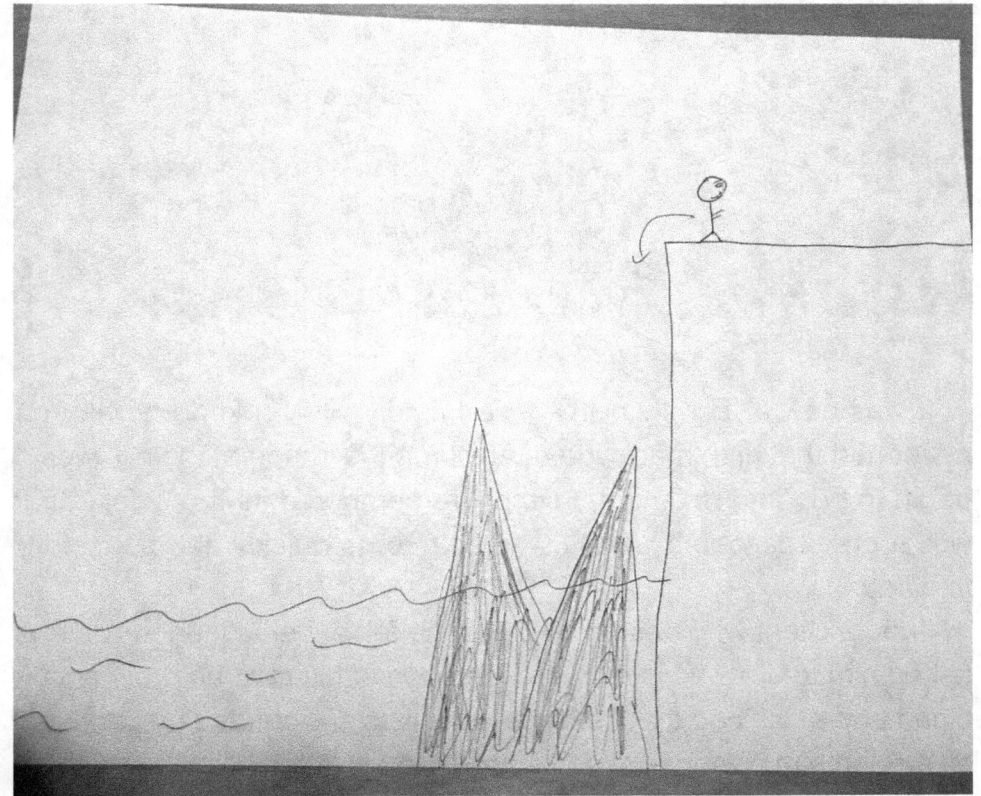

That happened until, one night, for whatever reason, I decided to do something I had never done before. In my mind, I decided to give the cliff a really funny-looking face and imagined that, every time someone got near it, it would say, "Hi there! How ya doin'?"

It was now a friendly cliff! And a friendly cliff could do no harm. I never had that nightmare again. Any time the image of the cliff would begin to pop into my mind, I simply remembered its funny face that would greet passersby, and I was able to go quickly and peacefully to sleep.

I had a client who described a fear he felt of being judged. When I asked him to draw a visual representation of his fear, he drew a dark cloud and explained that he felt as if he was surrounded by darkness all around him. When I asked him how he could turn it into something humorous, he looked at it for a moment and exclaimed, "Wait! That's my hair in the morning!!!!" He attached a head to the dark cloud, and suddenly it was nothing more than a ball of hair. I asked him if his hair could harm him, judge him, or keep him from progressing towards his goals, to which he responded, "Of course not!" I invited him, from that day forward, any time he began to feel judged, to imagine that the feeling was nothing more than his hair. To my knowledge, that fear never bothered him again.

Once you have established your clients' root fear, invite them to draw a picture of the fear. Explain that it doesn't have to be a masterpiece, but simply some sort of visual representation of what they have been feeling. Once finished, invite them to explain what they drew, and then verify, "When you see this image, do you feel fear?" Once they say yes, invite your clients to then modify their drawing to something silly or humorous. Only make suggestions if absolutely necessary; it is better for them to allow their own mind to come up with the new image. Once they have, invite them to describe the new image to you. Again, it should be something that's funny or goofy. Humor is the antidote of fear. It's difficult to laugh and feel fear at the same time. Once your clients have described the new image to you, explain that this is all that fear ever was. Ask, "Can (whatever their new image is) ever harm you?" Once they respond that it cannot, encourage your clients to remember this new image any time they feel the old fear creeping in. Once they've done so enough times, the fear will eventually be completely eradicated.

Bigger Than Your Fear

To perform this exercise, invite your clients to close their eyes and imagine that their fear is standing directly in front of them. Tell them to imagine that they have just swallowed a magic potion that causes them to grow indefinitely and their fear to shrink indefinitely. Tell them to continue to see themselves grow bigger and bigger, stronger and stronger, more and more powerful, and to see their fear growing smaller and smaller, tinier and tinier, until they can easily smash it with their foot, pick it up in their hands and flick it away, or simply blow their fear into oblivion.

Chapter 6: Breakthrough

Ten Seconds of Courage

Have you ever heard the term "paralysis by analysis"? This usually happens because a person believes that they lack the courage to complete a certain task. If you find that this is the case with one of your clients, this tool may be for you.

After utilizing one or more of the tools in this chapter to help your clients overcome the root of their fear, remind them that they really only need to be courageous for ten seconds at a time. If they feel impressed to reach out to someone, they only need to muster up ten seconds worth of courage, or enough courage to simply dial someone's phone number or approach someone to begin a conversation. Ten seconds doesn't seem like a long time, so this will usually alleviate the tension and get clients out of the paralysis by analysis mode. Invite them to repeat the words "ten seconds of courage!" any time they need a boost of confidence to take the action required to reach a certain goal.

The Mentor's Toolbox

Boxes

There will come a time when you sense that some clients may be hiding something from you or holding back information regarding a limiting belief that they need to eliminate. They may display closed-off body language by folding their arms or crossing their hands over their body. They might deflect probing questions that you ask by sharing a completely unrelated story instead of answering the question itself. When this happens, gently encourage your clients to actually answer the question, but if you can tell that there may still be something going on that they are hiding, use this exercise.

Chapter 6: Breakthrough

Draw a number of boxes on a sheet of paper and explain that our subconscious minds are made up of several different compartments or boxes. There is a box for money, a box for relationships, a box for spirituality, and so on. The purpose of mentoring is to explore the contents of each box and clean up or make adjustments when necessary. Unfortunately, occasionally we have a box that we like to sit on. Draw a person sitting on top of one of the boxes with their arms folded and an unhappy expression on their face. Explain that there can be times when we want to hide the contents of certain boxes from our mentors because we fear that opening and exploring those boxes will be painful, embarrassing, or shameful, but these are always the most important boxes to explore. Gently ask them, "What is in the box that you are sitting on?"

Your clients may get very quiet or emotional when you ask this question. Give them a moment to compose themselves and process the question. Send them love in your mind and reassure them that you are there to support them. Ask permission to talk about whatever it is. Show extreme kindness and acceptance. You will likely be diving into extremely personal issues. Continue to ask your clients' permission before going any further into the breakthrough process.

If your clients say that they don't know what is inside the box, simply say, "I know you don't know what's inside the box, but if you did know what was inside it, what would you say is there?" This is a simple tool to help a person get around the habit of saying the words "I don't know." You may also invite them to use the Mirror Exercise (page 73) to find out what is inside the box.

If your clients continue to resist and display stubborn energy, gently explain that you care about them. Ask them how serious they are about accomplishing their goals. If they say that they are very serious, help them understand that whatever is in this box is keeping them from achieving their goals as quickly as they would like. You are there to help. Remind them that they are safe with you and that there will be no judgment. If appropriate, remind them that you are not their religious leader and that they do not have to give any details that they do not wish to share, but that you would love to help them through whatever it is so that they can move forward and progress more quickly. Then kindly ask, "May we explore the contents of this box?"

When they are ready to talk about it, listen attentively to whatever they share. Use whatever additional tools you feel impressed to use to help them achieve a breakthrough.

Chapter 6: Breakthrough

The Wall

There will be times when your clients feel stuck. Sometimes they may even say that they have hit a wall with their progress. Subconscious walls are interesting because they obstruct a person's view of their goals. If they can't visualize themselves achieving their goals, they probably won't. You will need to help your clients bring the wall down so that they can "see" better.

When clients use this kind of language, give them a sheet of paper and invite them to draw a visual representation of the wall. Pay close attention to what they draw. Once they are finished, ask them to identify what the wall is made out of in their mind. Is it made of wood, concrete, bricks? The most common answer is bricks, and if so, have them draw in the individual bricks in the wall. Then ask them if all of the bricks represent several layers of the same limiting belief, if each layer of bricks represents a different limiting belief, or if each individual brick represents a separate limiting belief. Have them label what each brick, row of bricks, or the wall itself represents. In some cases, this may be fear, self-doubt, feelings of inadequacy, etc. This may seem daunting to them, especially if the wall that they feel is there is extremely tall. They will probably not have attempted to work on bringing the wall down because of how daunting a task it appears to be.

This is where the fun begins.

If it is indeed made of bricks in their drawing, share with them that the only thing that needs to be removed from a brick wall to bring the entire wall down is the bottom layer of bricks. The bottom layer supports the rest of the bricks, so if they are removed, the entire wall comes crashing down. This often brings about a great sense of relief to the clients as they realize that removing their subconscious block isn't such a daunting task after all. All you have to do now is address whatever the bricks at the bottom layer represent, utilizing one or more tools in your toolbox.

If your clients say that the wall is made of stone, concrete, or anything that is completely solid, that usually means that it represents one single deeply rooted emotion or limiting belief. Invite them to identify what it represents and then use the appropriate tool to help them bring the wall down once and for all.

Chapter 6: Breakthrough

Limiting Beliefs

A *limiting belief* is any belief that keeps you from taking the necessary action to achieve your greatness. Some examples may include:
I can't afford it . . .
I'm not good enough . . .
Money is the root of all evil . . .
I'll never have that . . .
That just isn't in the cards for me . . .
I'm too old/young/fat/skinny/tall/short, etc.
I don't have the time . . .

Throughout their journey to success, your clients will come face-to-face with limiting beliefs. There will come a time when they will need to make a choice between their limiting beliefs and their results. They cannot have both. When limiting beliefs surface, assure your clients that they are not alone in feeling them. The following tools are designed to remove limiting beliefs from the mind and replace them with positive, empowering beliefs.

The Mentor's Toolbox

Limiting Beliefs Purge

It is common for fears, doubts, and limiting beliefs to surface in our minds when we focus on a goal. When fears, doubts, or limiting beliefs come to their mind, invite your clients to write them down on a piece of paper and then destroy the paper by tearing it up, shredding it, or burning it. This removes whatever it is from their head and puts it onto something that they can then discard. This sends a message to your clients' subconscious that they are the one in control.

Chapter 6: Breakthrough

Limiting Beliefs to Positive Beliefs

Invite your clients to draw a vertical line down a sheet of paper to create two columns. On the left side, invite your clients to make a list of their top ten to twenty limiting beliefs. Once this is completed, instruct them to write the positive opposite of each limiting belief on the right side of the paper plus an additional positive statement. For example, if the limiting belief is "I am too old to get rich," the positive opposite might be "I am the perfect age to get rich," and a supplemental positive statement could be "and I get richer each day," making the full statement "I am the perfect age to get rich, and I get richer each day." The positive opposite statement neutralizes the limiting belief, and the additional positive statement causes the brain to focus on the more empowering belief. Instruct your clients to do this with all of the limiting beliefs they wrote down on their paper. Once they have done this, invite them to tear the paper down the middle and destroy the left side (the limiting beliefs) by tearing, shredding, or burning it, and then repeat the positive beliefs as affirmations. Repeat this process for seven to thirty consecutive days.

Belief Breakthrough

(As taught by Kris Krohn and the founders of Limitless, used with permission.)

Belief Breakthrough is designed to create awareness of any limiting beliefs that may be negatively impacting a person's results in life. The focus of this process is to exchange negative beliefs with positive beliefs in order to improve a person's happiness and results.

GUIDELINES FOR BELIEF BREAKTHROUGH: The following guidelines are important to consider when performing Belief Breakthrough.

1. Participants should be aware that the breakthrough processes often include exploring the inception of a negative belief. Volunteers may be invited to share the circumstances surrounding the creation of a limiting belief. Often the circumstances of a negative belief include a perceived traumatic event, whether real or imagined.
2. The title of "mentor" or "belief breakthrough coach" does not indicate a professional therapeutic license or degree. It designates someone who has been trained in and has demonstrated consistent ability to follow the scripts to replace negative, false, or limiting beliefs with positive and empowering beliefs.
3. Belief Breakthrough work is often cited for mending relationships, improving income, and even supporting participants in taking positive steps to improve their own health. Use of Belief Breakthrough is strictly for education, self-improvement and life enhancement. No medical advice or claims are offered in any way. I, and my company, Feel Well, Live Well, its facilitators and parent organization offer no medical, therapeutic, diagnostic or curative treatments, and make no medical claims, whether for improving, treating, or curing any medical condition.

4. Feel Well, Live Well does not encourage public confession or disclosure of personal information that would normally only be discussed in a confidential setting such as with a psychologist, psychiatrist, or religious leader.
5. Feel Well, Live Well advocates that the participant does not need to confront any individual to experience a breakthrough or overcome a challenge. Feel Well, Live Well teaches that problems lie within us and within our perceptions. Confronting another person is never required for an individual to alter their negative beliefs or improve their perceptions.
6. Confidentiality must be maintained for the protection and privacy of the participant. Unless the breakthrough coach has express permission from a participant, breakthrough sessions must remain confidential. For training or example purposes and in the proper setting, generalities of a session may be shared without disclosing personal details. We encourage breakthrough coaches to practice professional ethics.
7. Note: If you would like to experience Belief Breakthrough on a greater level, consider attending Limitless. Should you choose to become a certified belief breakthrough coach, consider registering for the Limitless Inner Circle Program. This program is separate from Feel Well, Live Well and is owned by a separate company. All transactions would take place directly through them.

Belief Breakthrough Script

Step 1: Ground

"Do I have permission to facilitate this breakthrough? Great. I'm going to invite you to close your eyes and ground."

Use deep breathing with your eyes closed to get into a meditative state. The purpose of grounding is to disconnect from your thoughts and connect to your intuition. Clear your mind of all thoughts and prepare to receive answers.

Step 2: Identify a Limiting Belief
"What is the number one limiting belief coming up for you?"

Listen for the intuitive answer. Trust that whatever comes up is exactly what you need to work on in this moment, especially if it doesn't seem to make sense.

Step 3: Explore Your Memories
"What is the first memory that comes up for you when you think this thought?"

Trust that whatever memory arises is the perfect place to focus your breakthrough work. If they hesitate, ask if they feel comfortable sharing the memory with you. You can still complete the process even if they don't vocalize the memory.

Step 4: Identify the Deeper Limiting Belief
"What did you decide about yourself when you experienced this?"

What comes from this is the deeper belief that you found in Step 2 and is the one you really need to work with.

Step 5: Examine the Cost of the Limiting Belief
"Go ahead and open your eyes. What is the cost of believing this thought?"

Chapter 6: Breakthrough

Examine how this belief is showing up in your life. How has it affected your results in the past and present? How will it affect you in the future if you don't change it? Consider how it impacts other aspects of your life, including finances, physical health, relationships, and personal power.

Step 6: Give Yourself Permission to Shift
"Are you ready to get out of this limiting belief and into one that empowers you?"

Consciously choose to shift your beliefs and make a change.

Step 7: Create a New Belief
"Let's explore a new belief that will serve you better . . . "

Make the choice to change your old limiting belief to a new, empowering belief that will serve you better. State the new belief in first person and in the present tense.

Step 8: Rewrite Your Story
"I am going to invite you to close your eyes again and to go back to this memory. If you could invite anyone into this moment to show up for you and support you, who would that be? Great, let's invite them in. What is the first thing that happens as they step into this memory? What words are they sharing with you?"

Go back to the original memory from which you created your false belief. Imagine reinterpreting the experience in a way that serves you better and that is more aligned with the truth of the new belief. If necessary, solicit in your imagination the help of your higher self or someone who you deeply trust to support and assist you in rewriting your story. What words of support, encouragement, love, wisdom, and power would they offer to help you heal the pain of this experience and rewrite your story?

Step 9: Claim Your New Belief

"Repeat after me . . . (state the new belief). Let's find the best way for you to celebrate this choice. What are your next steps by making this new choice? Congratulations!"

Repeat the words of their new chosen belief. Shift the energy and emotion anchored to the memory to a strong positive emotion. Speak the words of their new belief they chose. State the new belief out loud with confidence, conviction, and power. Say it repeatedly. Declare it in the way that feels the most authentic to you. Commit to living this new belief and finding evidence to support it. Find a way to help them celebrate this new belief in the memory that came up or in their present life. A great way to end the breakthrough session is to ask for their next steps with the new choices they are now making.

Chapter 6: Breakthrough

Personal Breakthrough

Step 1: Ground

Use deep breathing with your eyes closed to get into a meditative state. The purpose of grounding is to separate from your thoughts and connect to intuition. Clear your mind of all thoughts and prepare to receive answers.

Step 2: Identify a Limiting Belief

"What is the number one limiting belief coming up for me?"

Listen for the intuitive answer. Trust that whatever comes up is exactly what you need to work on in this moment, especially if it doesn't seem to make sense.

Step 3: Explore Your Memories

"What is the first memory that comes up when I think this thought?"

Trust that whatever memory arises is the perfect place to focus your breakthrough work.

Step 4: Identify the Deeper Limiting Belief

"What did I decide about myself when I experienced this?"

What comes from this is the deeper belief that you defined in Step 2. This is the one you really need to work with.

Step 5: Examine the Cost of the Limiting Belief

"What is the cost of believing this thought?"

Examine how this belief is showing up in your life. How has it affected your results in the past and present? How will it affect you in the future if you don't change it? Consider how it impacts other aspects of your life, including finances, physical health, relationships, and personal power.

Step 6: Give Yourself Permission to Shift
Consciously choose to shift your beliefs and make a change.

Step 7: Create a New Belief
Make the choice to change your old limiting belief to a new, empowering belief that will serve you better. State the new belief in first person and in the present tense.

Step 8: Rewrite Your Story
Revisit the memory where you created your false belief. Imagine reinterpreting the experience in a way that serves you better and that is more aligned with the truth of the new belief. If necessary, solicit the help of your higher self or someone whom you deeply trust to support and assist you in rewriting your story. What words of support, encouragement, love, wisdom, and power would they offer to help you heal the pain of this experience and rewrite your story?

Step 9: Claim Your New Belief
Shift the energy and emotion anchored to the memory to a strong positive emotion. State your new belief out loud with confidence, conviction, and power. Say it repeatedly. Declare it in a way that feels most authentic to you. Commit to living this new belief, and find evidence to support it. Find a way to celebrate this new belief in the memory that came up or in your present life. A great way to end the breakthrough is to determine your next steps with the new choices you are now making.

Original Belief Breakthrough script by Kris Krohn. Shared with permission.

Chapter 6: Breakthrough

Neuroassociation Change

Our brains associate absolutely everything in our lives with one of two things: pain or pleasure. Our subconscious mind's primary function is to keep us alive, so it puts up red flags to help us avoid anything that it thinks will cause us pain. For example, have you ever known someone who wanted to release weight and get fit but didn't because they believed that the process of doing so would be too uncomfortable? Change doesn't happen until the perceived pain of the change process becomes less than the pain of staying the same. Throughout your career as a mentor, you will likely work with clients that have neuroassociations that need to be altered. The following tool may be beneficial if you are working with someone who wants to become financially wealthy but subconsciously associates money and the process of becoming wealthy with pain.

There is a three-step process to helping a person change a neuroassociation. Before you begin, you should always ask your clients' permission to do something outside the box. Let them know that you are about to walk them through a process which may seem unusual to them in order to help shift their neuroassociation. Only proceed if they give you permission.

Step 1: Interruption

Each time you think about something that you associate with pain, the neurons fire inside your brain and send signals all throughout your nervous system as a warning. You must interrupt this process while it is taking place. To do this with clients, invite them to talk about the pain of whatever it is that you are discussing. For example, if your clients want to break a painful neuroassociation regarding money, invite them to describe in great detail an experience that they had that gave them evidence that money caused pain. Instruct them to really allow themselves to feel the negative emotions that they felt during the experience. As they begin to talk about the experience, watch their countenance. About ten seconds into their story, suddenly do something to cause them to lose their train of thought. You might startle them, you might say, "Stop! Stand up, twirl around ten times and then sit back down." You might even throw water in their face. This causes what is called a pattern interrupt and momentarily stops the painful neurons in their brain from signaling. Have you ever been deep in a conversation with someone, when something catches your attention momentarily, and when you turn back to the person that you were talking to, you ask, "Wait, what was I just talking about?" Whatever caused your momentary distraction also caused the neurons in your brain to stop firing as they had been, causing a very real pattern interrupt. You'll know that you have done this effectively when you ask your clients to continue talking about the experience that they were sharing and they won't be able to because they can't remember how it felt. This may take a few tries, meaning you may need to have your clients start and stop their story several times and interrupt them several times before they finally get to a point where they no longer feel the pain of what they were saying. Once this interruption phase has taken place, proceed to the next step.

Step 2: Replacement

Now that you have interrupted a painful neuroassociation, you must help your clients form a new neuroassociation, linking whatever it is to high amounts of pleasure. Invite your clients to think about whatever it is that they are shifting. For example, if you are working on money, invite them to think about money, or better yet, have them hold some money in their hands. While they are doing so, they must experience something that would bring them pleasure. For example, my wife and I both love chocolate. When we did this exercise with money, we bought some high-quality chocolate and ate it while holding hundred-dollar bills. Again, once you've done the interruption phase of this tool, invite your clients to think about whatever it was that was causing them pain while doing something that brings them pleasure, such as eating chocolate or receiving a brief massage, or whatever it may be. Again, the key here is to replace the old painful neuroassociation with a pleasurable one. You want them to associate money, or whatever it is, with the pleasure of eating chocolate, getting a massage, or whatever is pleasurable to them. Repeat this step until your clients can think of whatever used to cause them pain and associate it with pleasure.

Step 3: The "Why"

Ask your clients what this new outlook will do for them and how making this change will impact their life. It is important that your clients continue to focus on the purpose of changing their neuroassociation for the change to be permanent. If their why isn't great enough, they may slip back into old ways of thinking.

To recap, the process of helping someone change their neuroassociation has three steps: 1) interruption; 2) replacement; and 3) focusing on the "why."

Soul Wounds

Soul wounds are emotional scars that have formed because of particularly traumatic experiences that a person has had. Different emotions are stored in different parts of the body, so a person can have multiple soul wounds throughout the body. For example, if a person has been sexually abused, they will more than likely have soul wounds in their gender areas. If a person was constantly told when they were young to shut up or made to feel like their opinion didn't matter, they will likely have a soul wound in their throat near their vocal cords. If you sense that your clients may have some soul wounds, invite them to draw a rough outline of a body, which will represent them. Next, invite them to check in with intuition and then make markings on the paper inside the body they drew in all areas where they feel they have soul wounds. Once this is done, invite your clients to label each soul wound with what they feel caused it. For example, they might label a soul wound in their right wrist "age five, reaching for the cookie jar and had my wrist smacked with a ruler by my dad, who told me I can't have the things that I want," and so forth.

Next, invite them to look over their paper and write down everything their soul wounds caused them to believe about themselves, or in other words, what limiting beliefs these experiences taught them. Once they've done this, ask them if all of the limiting beliefs that they wrote down can be summed up into one major limiting belief that encompasses them all. If they say yes, ask them to identify the experience that caused them to accept this major limiting belief. You may find that using the Neuroassociation Change tool and/or the Belief Breakthrough script would be the most appropriate. If they say no, ask them to identify and write down all of the negative feelings associated with the limiting beliefs

Chapter 6: Breakthrough

that they wrote down. Once they've done so, ask them to pinpoint the first time they felt any one or a combination of those negative feelings. Once they have, ask, "If you no longer felt those negative feelings and were able to turn those limiting beliefs into more empowering ones, would your soul wounds heal?" Usually the answer will be yes, at which point you may proceed to the following tool: Timeline Breakthrough.

Timeline Breakthrough

Timeline Breakthrough is one of the deepest, most powerful and cleansing breakthrough techniques in the world. It combines elements of hypnotherapy, timeline therapy, NLP, and belief breakthrough. Because it is such a deep experience, I usually do not recommend using this tool when meeting with clients for the first time. Unless you have built an extremely high level of rapport and know the person will be able to handle and value this level of breakthrough, I suggest waiting until after you've already met with them several times. To begin, ensure that your clients are sitting in a comfortable position and invite them to completely clear their mind while taking a couple of deep breaths in and exhaling through their mouth. Then use the following script:

What is the number one negative emotion or limiting belief that is keeping you from reaching your greatest potential?

How is this showing up in your life?

If you were to tap into your intuition and ask what that is costing you, including a specific dollar amount, what answer comes to you? (Once they specify a dollar amount, ask them to specify if that is the amount it is costing them per year, per month, per day, etc.).

Is hanging onto _____ (the negative emotion or limiting belief) serving you?

Are you willing and ready to make a change?

Is it all right with your unconscious mind for you to release (the limiting belief or emotion) today and for you to be aware of it consciously?

Chapter 6: Breakthrough

Please take a deep breath in through your nose and blow it out through your mouth, close your eyes, and allow yourself to clear your mind and become completely present.

What is the root cause of this problem, the first time you felt this way, or the first event in your life which, when disconnected, will cause the problem to disappear? If you were to tap into your intuition, was it before, during, or after your birth?
BEFORE: In the womb or before?
WOMB: What month?
BEFORE: Was it from pre-earth life, or was it passed down to you genealogically?
PRE-EARTH LIFE: How long before you came to Earth?
GENEALOGICALLY: How many generations ago?
AFTER: How old were you?

That's right. Now, in just a moment, I am going to ask you to see the timeline of your life. Each of us has a timeline of our lives, and each of us has a direction that we perceive our past and future. For example, some people perceive their past to their left and their future to the right. Others perceive their past behind them and their future in front of them. If you were to ask your intuition which direction it perceives your past, in which direction would you point? Go ahead and point in that direction now.

That's right. And which direction does your intuition perceive your future?

Beautiful. Now, in your mind, float up above the timeline of your life and back to the event that you described, but make sure that you are high and far enough back so that you can see the event below you but can no longer feel the emotions from that event. Please let me know when you are there.

Excellent. Now see a giant drain forming at the bottom of this event, and down it goes all of the negative emotion that was present at this event and any event like this that took place all the way up to the present moment. Tapping into your intuition, how many times have you felt this emotion(s)/limiting belief(s) from that moment until now?

See _____ (the number) giant drains forming at the bottom of each and every event in your life in which you felt _____ (the emotion/limiting belief). Let me know when you can see that. What does that look like? What does that sound like? What does that feel like?

Watch as every ounce of this limiting belief/emotion, both from these events and any other negative emotions that are still inside you, gets sucked down this drain and into nothingness until they are completely gone while still preserving the lessons from each of these events. And as it drains, I invite you to choose someone that you love and trust to float up to meet you above your timeline and deliver a message to you that will help you learn the lessons from these events. Remember, every event that we experience is designed to teach us specific lessons and give us experience. If you could ask absolutely anyone, who would it be?

Beautiful. See _____ (the person's name) floating up to meet you in the air above your timeline. Feel them embrace you and see them look you in the eyes. And, speaking as if you were _____ (the person's name) out loud to you, what message would _____ (the person's name) relay to you?

Chapter 6: Breakthrough

That's right. And what lessons do you choose to learn, the learning of which will help you let go of this emotion/limiting belief once and for all?

That's right. Anything else? That's right. Breathe all of those lessons in and allow them to become a part of you. Beautiful. Now look down at the event, and let me know once all of the negative emotion has completely drained.

Excellent. Now float down inside the event and look around. What emotions are present now?

That's right. Can you now feel gratitude for these experiences, for all of the lessons that they allowed you to learn?

Now, float back up above your timeline and float back towards the present moment, checking to make sure that the emotions are completely gone from all subsequent events that took place from that first event until now and preserving all of the lessons that you learned. If you find any more emotion, form another drain under the event and watch it all get sucked down into nothingness until it is completely gone, and if there are more lessons to learn, please speak them out loud. Once you have done this, float back to now, and open your eyes when you are finished.

Now, can you remember any event in the past where you used to be able to feel that limiting belief/emotion, and go back and notice if you can feel it, or you may find that you cannot. Good, now come back to now.

Way to go! What did that do for you?

The Mentor's Toolbox

How will this affect your future?

What is a specific action step that you can set for yourself to further integrate this change in your life?

Excellent. Way to go!!

CHAPTER 7
CONNECTION

The Mentor's Toolbox

To one degree or another, most people struggle with perfectionism, doubt, and/or lack of self-esteem. The key to overcoming these tendencies is to raise your personal value. The tools in this chapter will help you to do so, both in your own life and in the lives of your clients.

Chapter 7: Connection

Receiving Compliments

Have you noticed how difficult it can be for some people to genuinely receive compliments? If someone gives them one, they brush it off or immediately turn it around and bounce it right back at the other person.

This tool works best if you are doing group mentoring. If you are teaching a class with several people, invite your clients to, on a voluntary basis, come to the front of the room and inform them that they are not allowed to do anything during this exercise except look into the eyes of the other participants and say "thank you." They are not allowed to return the compliment. Have your volunteers line up and, one by one, approach another participant, look them in the eyes, and give them a sincere compliment. Then invite everyone in the line to form a circle around your clients and give them a group hug.

If you are alone with your clients, have them stand in front of a mirror and give themselves compliments. Watch their body language to gauge when they have a shift. You will notice the shift when they finally relax and become comfortable giving themselves love.

One Thousand Reasons

If you can tell that your clients struggle with self-esteem, invite them to make a list of one thousand reasons why they like themselves. Yes, one thousand reasons, and yes, this may take a while, and that's OK! Doing this can do wonders for your clients' self-worth.

Chapter 7: Connection

I AM ENOUGH Poster

If you want to take it to another level, invite your clients to get a large poster board and write the words I AM ENOUGH at the very top and then prop the poster board up in a place that they frequently walk by, such as a bedroom door or an office door. Every time they pass by, they must write in teeny tiny letters something that they like about themselves, and they must continue to do so until the entire poster board is completely filled. This is called an I AM ENOUGH poster.

The Greatness I See in You

If you have an even number of clients in the room, invite them to find a partner and to choose a partner A and a partner B. Instruct them that when you say "go," partner A will have sixty seconds to look directly into partner B's eyes and, using the entire time, complete the following statement: "The greatness I see in you is . . ." Meanwhile, partner B can say nothing and may only allow Partner A to look into their eyes and complete the statement. After sixty seconds have passed, partner B then takes a turn completing the same statement. This is an amazing way to end a class because of how uplifting it can be. Encourage them to partner up with someone they do not know and, if appropriate, invite them to link hands or arms with their partners. They may be shocked at how much greatness they can see in their partners and how much their partners see in them. I would encourage you to actually do this exercise with yourself while standing alone in front of a mirror.

Chapter 7: Connection

The Mirror Appreciation Exercise

As taught by Jack Canfield in the manual of his Breakthrough to Success seminar. Used with permission.
1. Say your name
2. Appreciate yourself for:
    a. Achievements, successes, risks taken
    b. Disciplines kept
    c. Temptations overcome
3. Say "I love you" to yourself
4. Take it in (receive it), breathe

The mirror exercise is one of the simplest, yet most powerful self-esteem and self-confidence building exercises in the world. Its purpose is to replace the normal negative self-talk that dominates our thoughts with positive self-affirming self-talk. It is an exercise that should be performed every night for forty days.

Every night before going to bed, stand in front of a mirror and appreciate yourself for all that you accomplished throughout the day. Start with a few seconds of looking into the eyes of the person in the mirror—your mirror image of yourself looking back at you. Then start by saying your name, followed by appreciating yourself (out loud) for the following things:

1. Any achievements (business, financial, educational, personal, emotional, etc.)
2. Any personal disciplines you kept (exercise, meditation, prayer, dietary, etc.)
3. Any temptations that you did not give in to (dessert, lying, breaking commitments, etc.)

The Mentor's Toolbox

Maintain eye contact with yourself throughout the exercise. When you are complete, end by continuing to look deep into your own eyes and say, "I love you." Then stand there for another few seconds to really feel the impact of the experience as if you were the one in the mirror who had just listened to all of this appreciation. The trick during this last part is to not turn away from the mirror feeling embarrassed or thinking of yourself/the exercise as stupid.

Example: Here is an example of what it might sound like:

"Jack, I want to appreciate you for the following things today: First, I want to appreciate you for going to bed on time last night without staying up too late watching TV; you got up bright and early this morning, and had a really good conversation with Inga. Then you meditated for twenty minutes before showering. You helped with preparing the kids' lunches and ate a healthy, low-fat, low-carbohydrate breakfast. You got to work on time and led a great staff meeting with your support team. You did a fantastic job of helping everyone listen during the staff meeting with your support team. You did an awesome job of helping everyone listen to the diverse feelings and ideas within the team. And you were great at drawing out the quiet ones. Let's see . . . Oh, and then you ate a really healthy lunch: soup and salad—and you didn't have the dessert that was offered! And you drank the ten glasses of water that you committed to drinking every day. Congratulations on that one! . . . And you stayed in a good mood all day today. You didn't let other people's problems become your own. It would have been easy to let Deborah's complaints get to you, but you didn't. You were able to not feel personally responsible for what happened to her. And you didn't take anything she said personally. Good job! And then let's see . . . You finished editing the new staff orientation manual, and you got a really good start on scheduling the summer management train-

Chapter 7: Connection

ing program. And then you filled in your Daily Positive Focus Form before you left work. Oh, and you appreciated your assistant for all of her contributions for the day. It was great to see how she just lit up. And when you got home, you spent quality time playing with the kids—especially Christopher—and read a book to all of them before bed. That was really special. And now you're going to bed at a good time again and not staying up all night surfing the net. You were great today . . . And one more thing: I love you!"

It is not unusual to have a number of the following reactions the first few times you do this: feeling silly, embarrassed, wanting to cry (or actually crying), or generally feeling uncomfortable. People have occasionally even reported breaking out in hives, feeling hot, sweaty, or a little light-headed. As this is a very unfamiliar thing to be doing, these reactions are natural and normal. We are not trained to acknowledge ourselves. In fact, we are mostly trained to do the opposite: "Don't toot your own horn." "Don't get a swelled head." "Don't get a stuffed shirt." "Pride is a sin." As you begin to treat yourself in a more positive and nurturing way, it is natural to have physical and emotional reactions as you release the old negative self-judgments, unrealistic expectations, parental wounds, and so forth. If you experience any of these feelings—and not all people do—don't let them stop you. They are only temporary and will pass after a few days of doing the exercise.

Note: If you find yourself lying in bed, and you realize you haven't done the exercise, get out of bed and do it. The part of looking at yourself in the mirror is an integral part of the exercise. Remember: you will only get as much out of this exercise as you put into it.

One last bit of advice: If you live with someone (spouse, housemate, children, parents), let them know in advance that you will be doing this exercise each evening for a month or so. You do not want them to walk in on you while you are doing it and think you have lost it!

Heart Tap

Do you ever find yourself stuck in your head? Do you worry about what people will think about you before you give presentations or begin mentoring appointments? Sometimes, the simple act of gently tapping on your heart can bring you out of your head and into your heart. Make sure to teach your clients this principle if they regularly give public presentations.

Chapter 7: Connection

Heart Meditation

Below is the script for my heart meditation. For best results, encourage your clients to record it in their own voice and listen to it first thing in the morning, before a job interview, before a presentation, or any time they feel that they are getting caught in their heads rather than in their hearts:

Take a deep breath in and exhale through your mouth. And as you do, focus your breathing on your heart. Breathe deeply into your heart. Close your eyes, and focus all of your attention on your heart. Go now and allow yourself to be one with your heart. And as you allow yourself to breathe deeply into your heart and be one with your heart, feel the strength, power, and beauty of your being.

Allow yourself to feel the beating of your heart and allow yourself to feel gratitude that your heart is beating. That you are alive. Consider that for a moment. You are alive; you have a body—you have a brilliant body that moves and functions and sees and hears and tastes and smells and connects. This body that was given to you as a gift from your Maker.

And now, as you continue your heart-focused breathing, remember a moment in your life during which you were totally and completely grateful. Perhaps this was a moment that you are proud of. Perhaps this was a moment that you met someone or connected with someone. Breathe in your heart while focusing on your heart and allow yourself to feel that wonderful, powerful moment, that magical moment. Feel how sacred that moment was and is. And allow yourself to feel total gratitude for that moment. What a gift that moment was! And go to that moment now.

Step fully into that moment and be present in it. See what you saw, hear what you heard, feel what you felt in that moment. And allow yourself to smile and be fully present. Notice your breathing. How do you breathe when you are in total and complete gratitude? Celebration is the highest form of gratitude, so allow yourself to internally celebrate this moment and all the other moments like this one.

And fill yourself up with this feeling of gratitude and celebration. As you feel this intense feeling of gratitude and celebration, press gently on your heart to anchor this feeling in, lock this feeling of gratitude and celebration in so that, from this moment forward, all you need do is gently press on your heart and you instantly and automatically feel gratitude and celebration.

Now think of a second moment in your life that you can truly celebrate. A moment that allows you to feel totally and completely grateful. And fully step into that moment. See what you saw, hear what you heard, and feel what you felt when you were in that moment. Notice your breathing as you continue to breathe deeply into your heart, feeling total and complete gratitude and celebration. Breathe that feeling in, deeply in through your heart, and press gently on your heart to anchor that feeling in. That beautiful feeling of gratitude and celebration from that special, magical moment. Fill yourself with that sacred feeling.

And continue breathing deeply into your heart and think of a third moment in your life during which you felt totally and completely grateful and thankful. Think of the beauty of that moment and all that that moment has done for your life. And go now to that moment and feel what you felt in that moment, see what you saw, and hear what you heard in that moment.

Allow yourself to be filled with that gratitude and celebration. Feel the love you have in your heart as you continue breathing deeply into your heart. Become totally and completely present in that moment allowing that feeling to spread throughout your entire body. And gently press your heart to anchor that gratitude and celebration in so that, from this moment forward, any time you press your heart you are filled with that incredible feeling of gratitude and celebration.

And continuing in this state, in your heart, stay out of your head and stay in your heart, continue to breathe deeply into your heart, feeling grateful, consider this incomplete equation in your life, that situation that has unfinished business that has showed up in your life multiple times. And in this beautiful state of gratitude, ask yourself what do you need to focus on to complete the equation and solve the issue? And stay in your heart, and simply allow ideas to flow through you. Your heart knows the answer. Your heart knows all the answers.

Ask yourself what do I need to focus on, remember, or do to resolve this once and for all in my life? And allow the answer to come to you. And breathe the answer in and allow yourself to feel completely grateful for that answer.

Celebrate having received this answer in your mind. Now speak these words: "I am confident! I've got this!" And keeping this state of gratitude, celebration, and confidence, open your eyes, write the answer down, and go make it happen.

Parts Integration

Have you ever had clients that felt "conflicted"? Like part of them really wanted to change, but the other part of them wanted to hold on to their limiting beliefs or sabotaging habits? Parts integration is a powerful NLP technique used to help people in that situation. It aligns the values of the different parts of the subconscious mind and creates harmony within, leaving your clients feeling whole, as if their minds are working *for* them instead of *against* them.

Ask your clients, "Is it OK with your unconscious mind for you to make a change today, and for you to be aware of it consciously?" Once your clients respond affirmatively, proceed with the following technique:

Begin by establishing your clients' unwanted behavior or indecision and then the two (or more) opposing parts in their mind: the part that wants change and the part that resists change or continues to create the problem.

Encourage your clients to extend their hands and place them about shoulder width apart by their waist (without actually resting them on their waist or on their chair) with their palms facing up. Let them know that, as you proceed with the exercise, their hands will naturally gravitate towards each other, and they should be careful not to try to facilitate or stop the process from happening. Invite them to envision both parts of their mind that they have identified, one in each palm of their hands. Invite your clients to focus on one of the parts first. Allowing your clients to tap into intuition, ask that part what its intention is for doing what it has been doing. Once your clients answer, ask, "For what purpose?" Repeat this question for whatever response your clients give until they arrive at a positive value, such as freedom, joy, love, etc. Repeat the process with the other hand, asking the intention of the other part. Continue to repeat the question "For what purpose" with whatever answer they give until they arrive at a similar positive value. As this process unfolds, their hands will naturally become closer and closer together. Continue doing this process until their hands have merged.

Draw attention to your clients that both parts actually desire the same things.

Next, invite your clients to ask each part what resources it has that would be useful to the other part in achieving the intention that they both desire, and then imagine both parts sharing said resources. Invite your clients to turn their hands toward each other and visualize the two parts begin to merge as their hands continue to move closer together. As they come together, create a third image that represents the integration of the two former parts. Invite your clients to visualize the new, integrated image into their bodies by placing both of their hands on their hearts, breathing in and absorbing this new experience of being whole.

Next, create a state change in your clients' minds to help their minds make the necessary updates facilitated by this technique. This is done by asking them a question that causes them to think about something completely different from what you have been focusing on up to that point. One of my favorite ways to do this is to ask them what they had for dinner the night before.

Ask your clients to then think about how they feel about the old issue now that they are a whole, integrated person and how they are going to approach the issue differently in the future. If they still do not feel fully confident about facing the situation, there may be yet another part that needs to be integrated. If this is the case, repeat this process until all parts have "had a say" and are all "playing for the same team."

The Mentor's Toolbox

CHAPTER 8
RELATIONSHIPS

The Mentor's Toolbox

In this chapter you will find powerful tools to use when mentoring couples.

Chapter 8: Relationships

Love Languages

Author Gary Chapman teaches that each of us has a "love language," or something that helps us to feel loved.

Gifts: For some, it honors and recharges them to receive gifts. On special occasions they love to unwrap presents or receive flowers and the like.

Acts of Service: For others, receiving acts of service helps them recharge. If they come home to a clean house and all the dishes are done, or the lawn is mowed, or the car is washed, or whatever, they absolutely love it. Sometimes they can actually recharge by giving service to other people.

Loving Touches: Some prefer loving touches. If they are in a relationship with someone, they will often like to be held and cuddled. One of the best ways for them to recharge is to get a massage.

Words of Affirmation: There are people whose love language is words of affirmation. They thrive on praise and loving words. For them, listening to meditation tracks that contain positive affirmations can go a long way.

Quality Time: Finally, there are those whose love language is quality time with their loved ones. These are the people that prioritize spending time with family and friends in fun, uplifting situations.

Invite the couple that you are working with to share their primary love languages and assess how much fulfillment they are receiving from their partner. Then invite them to set goals to more effectively meet each other's love languages.

It is also important to understand that, whatever a person's love language is, receiving the opposite is generally what can hurt them the most. For example, for someone whose love language is words of affirmation, words of negative criticism can be quite painful. For someone whose love language is acts of service, it can be extremely frustrating when they are counting on someone to do a job and they don't pull through, or if they perceive others as creating extra work for them. A lot of times people don't express to their loved ones what their love languages are, so they often go unmet.

Chapter 8: Relationships

One Hundred Reasons

This is a powerful tool to use when mentoring couples. Simply invite each person in the relationship to make a list of 100 reasons why they love and appreciate the other person. This can be especially effective if words of affirmation is the love language of one or both of those in the relationship. Make sure that they understand that each item that they list must be genuine, sincere, and in the present tense. If you do not explain this, some couples may say things like, "I appreciate that you ALWAYS take out the trash without being asked" in a way that is hinting at something that they would like to see happen but isn't currently happening. This can create greater resentment in the relationship rather than greater harmony—the exact opposite of what you are hoping to achieve.

Encourage your clients to focus on various aspects of their partner and the relationship, such as their physical attributes, intellect, parenting skills, how hard they work, special skills (such as playing an instrument or cooking), etc. They must complete this exercise in its entirety, meaning they may not stop until they reach 100 reasons, but they may write more if they would like. There is no limit to how many reasons they appreciate each other. Once they have completed their lists, invite your clients to read the lists to each other every day for seven days and then report back to you.

The Mentor's Toolbox

Three-Minute Eye Contact

The world we live in seems to be creating greater and greater disconnect between people. Very few people take the time to look each other in the eyes, even within their close relationships. During this exercise, invite your clients to stand in front of each other, take each other by the hands, and simply look each other directly in the eyes for three full minutes. Instruct them that they are not to break eye contact (other than natural blinking, of course), they are not to say anything, and to avoid giggling or any other behavior that would cause an emotional disconnect. Once the three minutes have passed, invite them to write down all of the positive characteristics that they recognized in their partner and then share what they wrote out loud. Use this exercise if the couple seems uncomfortable saying good things about each other.

Chapter 8: Relationships

Heart-to-Heart Hugs

Most people are never taught the proper way to hug. When they go in for a hug, they each move to the left with their right ears lining up. This creates a disconnect because their hearts do not line up. Others, particularly men, subconsciously feel the need to slap each other on the back when they hug, furthering the disconnect.

A proper hug is when both people shift to their right and allow their left ears to line up, allowing their hearts to be close to each other, and no back slapping. This creates connection and bonding between the two people, even if they are both men. Encourage participants to hug for ten seconds or longer at a time, twelve times or more per day.

Holding... Giggle, Giggle, Giggle, Giggle...

Occasionally, one or both partners would benefit from a pattern interrupt. When this takes place, encourage your clients to embrace each other in a hug and both say in unison, "Holding . . . giggle, giggle, giggle, giggle . . ." with both participants wiggling their shoulders in a silly way while saying, "Giggle, giggle, giggle, giggle." Encourage them to be as silly and goofy as they would like while saying "giggle." The message that is sent subconsciously is "I validate what you are going through and the need for an embrace, and now let's have fun and be silly because everything is OK." Repeat this process until both partners are smiling and/or laughing.

Chapter 8: Relationships

Feelings vs. Emotions

This is less of a mentoring tool and more of an overall rule to live by. It is important to differentiate between *feelings* and *emotions*. Emotions are the physical manifestation of a feeling, the energetic charge if you will. While it is good to share your feelings with your loved ones, it is not good to dump your *emotions* on other people.

Establish a rule with your clients that, any time one or both partners feel the need to have a discussion with the other, that they first go dump their emotions using the tools found in the emotional release section of this book. Make it very clear that other people are not for dumping their emotions. When people use other people for emotional dumping, the person doing the dumping ends up feeling better, but the one being dumped on now feels worse. In relationships, this often leads to long, drawn-out arguments as partners attempt to wade through layers and layers of emotion. When my wife and I were first married and didn't know any better, disagreements took hours to resolve. Now that we have the emotional release tools found in chapter three, when disagreements happen, we each release the emotion of the situation in private to focus on finding solutions faster. Disagreements that once took hours to resolve are now resolved in a few minutes.

It is also important to establish the rule that all disagreements stay private and are to be resolved solely within the relationship. I have seen many relationships sour and die because a disagreement will take place and one or both partners take to social media to air their grievances, or they call their parents or close friends to discuss it. Few things are as detrimental to a relationship as gossip. With the exception of you as their mentor and any other qualified professionals that they have chosen to help them, they do not discuss the negatives of their relationship with anyone other than themselves. On the other hand, they may discuss each other's positive traits with as many people as they would like. This helps to strengthen a relationship and boosts each other's confidence.

Chapter 8: Relationships

Five-Point Communication

Most relationship experts agree that good communication between couples is absolutely critical. Unfortunately, few people know the best ways to communicate to resolve conflict. This is a tool to teach the couples you mentor. It is a five-step process to use when disagreements arise.

Step 1: Laser Listening. This means that when one person in the relationship is talking, the other is attentive and sets aside any and all distractions. Eye contact is key, and interruptions are not permitted.

Step 2: Summarize. Once the person has finished expressing their feelings and the other has concluded laser listening, it is now their turn to speak. They must repeat in their own words what they heard their partner say. A good way to begin this step is by saying, "Thank you. If I'm understanding you correctly, you are saying . . . Is that right?"

Step 3: Validation. Most people don't want to be right when it comes to disagreements; they simply want to be validated. They want to feel that their opinion matters. After summarizing what the other partner said, now is the time to validate their feelings. A good way to begin this step is by saying, "I can understand where you are coming from . . ."

Step 4: Empathize. This is *not* where a solution is presented. Many women don't seek a solution to the issues they bring up to their husbands. They simply want their husbands to be emotionally involved in their lives, and this is the step where the husband (or the wife) gets to fulfill this request. After validating the other's feelings, a good next step is to say, "That must be extremely difficult/frustrating/hard/etc."

Step 5: Affirm love and gratitude. Ending with a "thank you" and "I love you" is the icing on the cake and can bring a couple closer together than they were even before the disagreement. Simply saying, "Thank you for bringing that to my attention. I love you so much!" can do wonders. The couple then switches roles, if necessary.

Chapter 8: Relationships

Personality Types

An important aspect of any long-term relationship is understanding the personality type of each partner and how each type functions best.

Dr. Taylor Hartman created the Color Code personality chart, which groups various personalities into four major types, as follows:

Red Personalities

Red personalities are the power wielders of the world and are extremely task-oriented. They use logic, vision and determination to get things done quickly and effectively. To a true red personality, task completion has nothing to do with emotion.

- **Possible Strengths**

Reds tend to be action-oriented, assertive, confident, decisive, determined, disciplined, independent, excellent leaders, highly logical in their thinking, productive, responsible, and proactive. Many company presidents and CEOs are red personalities because they know how to get things done.

- **Possible Limitations**

Red personalities often have to be right. They can come across as harsh and critical, even when they don't mean to be. Reds can be cheap. They may prioritize their work over their personal relationships. They can be poor listeners and find it difficult to empathize. They can also exhibit controlling and domineering traits. True red personalities very rarely take breaks because they are so driven, so motivated, and so task-oriented that they often believe that relaxing is counterproductive.

- **Recharge**

Red personalities *especially* need to make blue screen time a priority, even if it is just a few minutes here and there. They often find that being outside in fresh air can be very rejuvenating. If possible, doing some of their work outside, for example working on their laptops at the park, can be the best of both worlds. They are able to be productive and get rejuvenated at the same time. It is also especially important that they make sure they take time to eat and stay hydrated. When on vacation, amusement parks are often at the top of the list because they can still be constantly moving. Going on as many rides as possible allows them a sense of accomplishment.

Blue Personalities

Life is a sequence of commitments for blue personalities. They are highly perfectionistic and can be distrusting and prone to worry. They are complex, highly logical, and are often very opinionated. Blue personalities tend to see life as a series of patterns and thus are often extremely organized and excellent with numbers, data, and technology.

- **Possible Strengths**

Blues are steady, ordered and enduring. Blues love with passion. They bring culture and dependency to society and home. They are highly committed and loyal. They are comfortable in creative environments. They strive to be the best they can be and are extremely organized.

- **Possible Limitations**

Blues are often the most stubborn of the four personality types. They can be insecure and judgmental. Lacking trust, they find themselves unforgiving and resentful. They often fail at seeing the positive side of life. They want to be loved and accepted, constantly seeking understanding from others while often refusing to understand and accept themselves.

- **Recharge**

Because blues tend to be the organizers, it often benefits them to do activities that are organized for them. Their form of blue screen time may include going to a restaurant so that someone can organize, prepare, and clean up after their meal.

White Personalities

Motivated by peace and ensuring everyone else is happy, white personalities will do anything to avoid confrontation. Their only demands from life are the things that make them and others feel comfortable. They are highly intuitive and empathetic. While they have a tendency to be shy and introverted, white personalities often connect at a deeper level with people than the other personality types once given the chance.

- **Possible Strengths**

White personalities are kind, considerate, patient and accepting, and have very little ego. They are good at constructing thoughts that did not exist before, just from listening carefully and taking time to think things through. They can easily articulate their feelings and the feelings of others.

- **Possible Limitations**

White personalities don't commonly share what they are experiencing, understanding, or seeing. They won't express conflict. White personalities may be unwilling to set goals because they dislike working at someone else's pace. They can be somewhat self-deprecating.

- **Recharge**

White personalities are often able to recharge best by being extremely still. They tend to enjoy taking warm baths during times when they won't be disturbed. They benefit from going to the spa, receiving massages, and spending time in nature. They are often the type that, when they go on vacation, they want to go somewhere remote where they can relax and do absolutely nothing.

Yellow Personalities

Yellows are motivated by fun and excitement. They are here to have a great time. They love being the center of attention and are known for being spontaneous and optimistic. Yellow personalities love to make friends and are often extremely extroverted.

- **Possible Strengths**

Yellow personalities are enthusiastic, very persuasive, and tend to have a large network of friends and acquaintances. They are naturally spontaneous and are always looking for something new to do. Yellows know how to liven up even the dullest of moments, can be very fun to be around, and love to see the good in everything.

- **Possible Limitations**

Yellow personalities develop friendships easily but can be very self-centered, keeping them from forming meaningful relationships. They often have a lot of friends but only at a superficial level. Yellows may have difficulty being productive. They often procrastinate and can be extremely flaky. They aren't the most reliable when it comes to keeping their commitments.

- **Recharge**

Yellow personality types recharge by doing fun things. It can be difficult for a yellow personality to go on vacation with a white personality because the white personality will usually want to just sit, relax, and read a book, while the yellow personality will want to go explore, do fun activities, and have as many new and fun experiences as possible. Much like red personalities, amusement parks are great ways for yellow personalities to recharge and unwind because it is both extremely fun and they get to be constantly moving and interacting with other people.

So what do you do if two different personality types are married to each other if they want to go on vacation and have all of their needs met? Helping a couple figure this out with the information in this book can help you shine as a mentor.

My wife and I are basically polar opposites when it comes to personality types. I am mostly red/yellow, while she is mostly white/blue. We've found that cruises and all-inclusive resorts tend to work best for us because we get to do a fun, exciting, and engaging activity or excursion in the morning (which appeases my red and yellow personalities), have some relaxing downtime in the afternoon (which appeases my wife's white personality), and then have an amazing dinner and watch a great show (which, of course, are all organized and produced by the cruise line or resort, which appeases her blue personality).

Invite your clients to share their preferences when it comes to vacations and special occasions. Encourage them to create a plan that would appease and fulfill the personality types of both partners.

Role Reversal

This tool is used when you can tell that clients have resentment towards someone from their past stemming from a particular event or series of events. Invite your clients to stand and imagine the person towards whom they have resentment sitting in their chair. Then invite them to say everything they feel they need to say to that person, holding nothing back. Remind them that your office is a safe environment for such experiences and that there will be absolutely no judgment from you regarding what they express during this exercise, regardless of the verbiage that is used. If your clients' native language is not English, and they would normally speak to the other person in their native language, invite your clients to do this exercise in their native language to more accurately simulate a conversation between them and the person that they are imagining is in the chair. Once your clients have said all that they feel they need to say, invite them to imagine themselves sitting in the chair and to now address themselves as the person whom they were just speaking to. Invite them to say everything they feel they need to say from the other person's point of view. Then repeat the process, inviting your clients to "reverse roles" and speak from the other person's perspective until a breakthrough is achieved. Encourage your clients to "embrace" the other person and say, "Thank you for the lessons you helped me learn."

CHAPTER 9
HEALTH AND BODY FAT REDUCTION

The Mentor's Toolbox

Many of the tools found in this book are for strengthening one's mind. As a mentor, you understand the importance of consistently strengthening one's body. The tools found in this chapter can help your clients achieve their health goals. Always make sure to encourage your clients to consult with a licensed healthcare professional before beginning any diet or exercise program.

Chapter 9: Health and Body Fat Reduction

The Six Essentials

The developer of the Bio-Energetic Synchronization Technique and founder of Morter Health System, Dr. M.T. Morter Jr., maintains that there are six essential choices when it comes to taking care of ourselves, namely:

1) What we eat
2) What we drink
3) What and how we breathe
4) How we exercise
5) How we rest
6) What we think and feel

If your clients struggle with eating a healthy diet, invite them to begin to make small changes today. Encourage them to 1) eat more fruits and vegetables, reduce the amount of processed foods they eat (including refined sugars and flours), replace alcoholic and carbonated beverages with green smoothies (more about them on page 177); 2) focus on alkalizing their body through proper supplementation and drinking plenty of water; and 3) spend time in nature, exercise regularly, and get plenty of rest at night.

While all of these are important, Dr. Morter explains that the most important area of focus is what we think. Remember that thoughts are made up of energy and can actually lead to improved health or illness depending on what we focus on. Have you ever known a family where it seems like there is always someone sick? Do you think there's a pretty good chance that there may be what we like to call "stinkin' thinkin'" going on inside that family?

If your clients want their health to improve, start by focusing on the things that they like about themselves. Even if it's something as simple as "I'm still breathing." Encourage them to find things each day that they are thankful and grateful for and focus their energy on those things. Remind them that whatever they focus on expands, so the more they are thankful and grateful, the more they will receive to be thankful and grateful for. The more they show gratitude toward themselves and their bodies, the better their health will become.

Chapter 9: Health and Body Fat Reduction

The Void Principle

A mistake that many who are working on improving their health make is focusing solely on what they will subtract from their lives rather than what they will add to it. For example, most people agree that reducing the intake of refined sugar and flours, processed foods, alcohol, and tobacco can lead to improvement in health. Unfortunately, most people stop there.

Encourage your clients to focus more on adding good things rather than eliminating "bad" things from their life. For example, while they may set a goal to go a certain number of days or weeks without any refined sugar, encourage them to replace it with something good, such as an extra glass of water.

Whenever we avoid something, it creates exactly that: a void. Because our brain is trained to fill in empty spaces, it will naturally look for ways to fill that void. If we aren't careful, it may fill it in with something similar to what we just removed. This is why *replacing* things in our lives is preferable to avoiding things. For example, instead of simply setting a goal that says, "No refined sugars for seven consecutive days," a more productive goal could be, "Replace refined sugar with healthy, green smoothies for seven consecutive days." Doing so can actually reduce or eliminate cravings for whatever your clients are eliminating from their life because it has been replaced and no void is left.

This also applies if you have clients that want to slim down. Most people make the mistake of saying they are "losing weight." The brain naturally wants to find things that it loses, so encourage your clients to replace the verbiage of "losing weight" with "slimming down," "replacing body fat with lean muscle," "living a vibrantly healthy life," and so forth.

Alkalization

All chemical properties are measured against two extremes: acidic and alkaline. This is determined by a score on the pH scale which ranges from 0-14, 0 being extremely acidic, 7 being neutral, and 14 being extremely alkaline. The human body was designed to be slightly alkaline (7.35), but certain types of foods, beverages, and actions can influence the body's pH balance.

The unfortunate truth is that the majority of those living in the United States follow what has come to be known as the Standard American Diet (SAD), which consists of a lot of processed foods, refined flours and sugars, soft drinks, alcohol, and very little whole foods, such as fruits and vegetables. Symptoms of an overly acidic body can include headaches, fatigue, weight gain, arthritis, depression, muscle and joint pain, and more. Stress can also contribute to an overly acidic body due to the release of cortisol into the body.

If you are working with clients towards any sort of health goal, I strongly encourage you to make alkalizing their body a priority. This is achieved by helping them reduce stress via the emotional release tools found in chapter three, encouraging them to reduce the amount of refined and processed foods in their diet, and inviting them to increase their consumption of whole foods, such as organic fruits and vegetables. Alkalization can also be facilitated with proper supplementation. Many health and wellness companies sell products designed to alkalize and detoxify the body.

Make sure to alert your clients that they will likely go through a process of detoxification during the first week of switching from an acidic diet to an alkaline diet. Detox symptoms may include headaches, trouble sleeping, and flu-like symptoms. Remind them that it will be worth it in the long run. The next tool in this chapter will help to drastically speed up the process of alkalizing the body.

Chapter 9: Health and Body Fat Reduction

Green Smoothies

One of my favorite ways to alkalize my body and make sure I am drinking enough water is by consuming delicious green smoothies each day. This is a simple tool that you can encourage your clients to incorporate into their nutrition plans that will help them have more energy, boost their metabolisms, and increase their overall health.

A few guidelines when making green smoothies:

- It should not be fruit juice-based. Your base liquid for these smoothies will be filtered water. Fruit juice, especially from concentrate, is loaded with sugar and calories and can actually have the opposite effect of alkalization.
- The main ingredient will be dark green cruciferous vegetables, such as spinach and kale. They are the primary alkalizing component of the smoothie.

The following is one of the most delicious and effective smoothie recipes you can find.

(Recipe courtesy of SmoothieShred.com, Thomas Tadlock, M.S., author of *Miracle Metabolism*, shared with permission.)

Green Smoothie

Fill your blender three-fourths of the way full (packed) with organic spinach
Add filtered water until it just covers the spinach
Then add
1 ripe banana, 1 handful chia seeds, and 1 handful frozen pineapple
Fill the rest of the blender to the top with frozen mango
Blend on high for two minutes or until your desired texture

The Mentor's Toolbox

Following this recipe will ensure that you have a delicious, balanced smoothie that helps you stay hydrated, alkalize your body, and get your omega-3 fatty acids (from the chia seeds), which helps to boost the metabolism. Drink one full smoothie every day.

Please note that if you aren't used to drinking 64+ ounces of water each day, this will likely make you go to the bathroom more frequently. I recommend finishing your smoothie at least four hours before going to bed so that your bladder doesn't keep you awake at night. You will know that you are on track to alkalizing your body when your stool becomes regularly green.

Chapter 9: Health and Body Fat Reduction

Intermittent Fasting

Intermittent fasting is an eating pattern that is becoming more and more popular around the world for the many benefits it has on the body. It simply means fasting, or abstaining from food, for a certain period of time, and then consuming all calorie-containing foods during a small window of time.

The most common form of intermittent fasting is what is known as the 16/8 principle, meaning that one fasts for sixteen hours per day and then consumes their meals during an eight-hour "feeding" window. Assuming that your clients sleep eight hours per day, they would wait four hours after waking to consume their first meal and conclude their last meal of the day four hours before going to bed. Some people choose to use this tool in conjunction with eating two meals per day: one larger meal and one smaller meal. The first, larger meal is known as "the feast" and consists of 60% of the person's daily caloric intake needs. The second meal then consists of the remaining 40% of the person's daily caloric intake needs. If they need 2,000 calories per day to reach their health and fitness goal, their first meal would consist of approximately 1,200 calories, and the second would consist of 800 calories. Following this method allows people to eat large, enjoyable meals that keep them full and consist of foods that they love, without feeling like they have to deprive themselves. This method is especially helpful if the clients eat out regularly. They key here is consistency, tracking calories, and making sure not to binge or overeat during meals.

Tracking Calories

Whenever a person is working on slimming down or otherwise changing their overall physique, it is important that they achieve proper caloric intake and the right balance of macronutrients (protein, fat, and carbohydrates) in their diet. Invite your clients to download an app on their cell phone that makes this easy, such as MyFitnessPal, and to keep track of what they eat throughout the day. This will include the seemingly "insignificant" things that they snack on, such as a small handful of nuts, a couple of potato chips, a sip of soda, and the like. While these things may seem small, they can add up very quickly and cause your clients to exceed their recommended caloric intake for the day, so you want to encourage your clients to keep track of absolutely everything and then send you a screen shot of everything they've eaten and a screen shot of their overall macronutrients each day. Help your clients make adjustments when needed.

Chapter 9: Health and Body Fat Reduction

Exercise Program

One of the ways that you will create greater and more lasting change is by following a regular exercise program. This could include a variety of different activities, from weight training to walking, biking, and dancing. The healthier your body becomes, the more confident and well-balanced you will feel. Exercise also releases endorphins, which will help to reduce the stress that normally accompanies change. Get outside and connect with nature. You are encouraged to exercise for at least sixty minutes at least three times per week to set an example for your clients and then invite them to do the same.

You will likely work with a variety of people that have a wide range of experience when it comes to exercise. Some will already be actively involved in an exercise program that is serving them well. Others may not have actively exercised in a long time. If the latter is the case, invite your clients to answer the following questions:

The exercises I enjoy doing are . . .

I will benefit from regular exercise in the following ways . . .

The exercise program that I commit to doing from now on includes . . .

Like to Dislike

There may be times when clients report having "guilty pleasures," or specific unhealthy foods that they have difficulty giving up. For example, one of my clients reported that she typically "cheated" by eating sugar cookies with cream cheese frosting. We used the following tool to help her no longer enjoy said cookies, thus facilitating the achievement of her fitness goals.

Before beginning this process, help your clients identify specific foods they wish to give up. This will not work for categories of foods, such as "sweets." Next, ask, "Is it OK with your unconscious mind to make a change today and for you to be aware of it consciously?" If your clients don't actually desire to give up the specific food, this tool will not be effective. Once they say, "Yes," use the following script to help your clients overcome their cravings for unhealthy foods:

We are now going to use a tool called "Like to Dislike" to help you to distance yourself from specific unhealthy foods once and for all. This will require you to make a graph on a sheet of paper. On a blank page, make two columns and, at the top, label the one to the left "like" and the column on the right "dislike." Draw lines from left to right across both columns separating the two columns into seventeen rows. To the left of your two columns label the rows as follows: 1) black and white or color, 2) near or far, 3) bright or dim, 4) location, 5) size of picture, 6) with own eyes or through someone else's eyes, 7) focused or dim, 8) framed or panoramic, 9) still or moving, 10) auditory location, 11) direction, 12) internal or external, 13) loud or soft (kinesthetic), 14) feeling location, 15) feeling size, 16) feeling shape, and 17) feeling intensity. Once you are done creating this chart, you should have two columns and seventeen rows. Make a note that the first nine rows have to do with visual cues, rows ten to thirteen have to do with audi-

Chapter 9: Health and Body Fat Reduction

tory cues, and rows fourteen to seventeen have to do with kinesthetic cues. This exercise WILL NOT work unless you have created this chart, so please do this before continuing.

It should look something like this:

		Like	**Dislike**
Visual Cues	Black and White or Color		
	Near or Far		
	Bright or Dim		
	Location		
	Size of Picture		
	With Own Eyes or Through Someone Else's Eyes		
	Focused or Dim		
	Framed or Panoramic		
	Still or Moving		
Auditory Cues	Auditory Location		
	Direction		
	Internal or External		
	Loud or Soft		
Kinesthetic Cues	Feeling Location		
	Feeling Size		
	Feeling Shape		
	Feeling Intensity		

Excellent, now think of the food that you have struggled with, meaning whatever it is that you like but wish you did not. As you think about it, get a clear picture of it in your mind. Answer the following questions in your mind and write down your answers in the left, or "like" column. Go through this quickly without stopping to think about it.

Is the picture in your mind black and white or color? Write down your answer in the first row of the left column. Write down your answers for each of the following in their appropriate spaces. Is the picture you have in your mind near or far? Is it bright or dim? What is the location of the image in your mind? What is the size of the picture? Are you looking at it as if through your own eyes or as if it were through someone else's eyes? Is the picture focused or dim? Framed or panoramic? Is it still or moving?

Once you've written down your answers for the first nine questions, ask yourself, "Are there any sounds that are important?" If no, skip to question fourteen. If yes, answer the following: Where is the location of the sound? What direction is the sound going? Is the sound internal or external? Is it loud or soft?

Next, ask yourself, "Are there any feelings that are important?" If no, you can end there. If yes, proceed to ask the following questions: Where in your body do you feel the feeling? What is the size of the feeling? What shape is the feeling? How intense is the feeling?

Great job! Now clear the screen, meaning clear your mind. Now, can you think of something that is similar to the food you have struggled with but which you absolutely dislike? For example, if you are overcoming cravings for milk chocolate, something similar in color but that you might strongly dislike might be unsweetened baking chocolate. Choose something that is similar to the food you have struggled with but that you absolutely detest, and get a clear picture of whatever it is in your mind.

Now, answer the same questions for this new image as you did for what you are hoping to overcome, this time writing down your answers in the right column. Is this new picture in your mind black and white or color? Write down your answer in the first row of the right column. Write down your answers for each of the following in their appropriate spaces. Is the picture you have in your mind near or far?

Chapter 9: Health and Body Fat Reduction

Is it bright or dim? What is the location of the image in your mind? What is the size of the picture? Are you looking at it as if through your own eyes or as if through someone else's? Is the picture focused or dim? Framed or panoramic? Is it still or moving?

Once you've written down your answers for the first nine questions, ask yourself, "Are there any sounds that are important?" If no, skip to question fourteen. If yes, ask the following: Where is the location of the sound? What direction is the sound going? Is the sound internal or external? Is it loud or soft?

Next, ask yourself, "Are there any feelings that are important?" If no, you can end there. If yes, proceed to ask the following questions: Where in your body do you feel the feeling? What is the size of the feeling? What shape is the feeling? How intense is the feeling? Once you have that done, clear the screen, meaning again, clear your mind.

In a moment, when I say go, you will pull up the picture of the first image into your mind. See it exactly the way you first saw it. In just a moment, you are then going to take that image and change it to meet the description of the second image that you thought of, or the image of what you dislike, meaning that if what you like was black and white and what you dislike was in color, you will change the image of what you like from black and white to color. You will move the image of what you like from wherever it is that you currently see it to the location of where you saw the image of what you don't like, and so on and so forth.

Take a moment and read through the description of the image of what you don't like. Now, bring the image of what you like onto your mind, and when I saw go, modify it to match the description of what you don't like, starting with the location. Ready? Go! Project the image of what you like to the location of what you dislike. Watch it change into everything you dislike. Feel the feeling of dislike enveloping what you used to like. You now absolutely dislike that food you used to like.

Now, you know the sound that Tupperware makes when it seals? Just like that, lock that new image in place, lock it right in there—locking it into your mind that you now absolutely detest that old behavior or substance. That's right.

Clear the screen! Now take a second and think about what you had for dinner last night. Good job! Now, what about that food you used to like? How is it different? Imagine a time in the future when you might be tempted to partake of that substance or behavior. What happens? Great job!

CHAPTER 10
ADDICTION RECOVERY

Statistics show that nearly one in two people will struggle with some form of addiction in their life. This may be an addiction to sugar, alcohol, tobacco, gambling, pornography, or even to negative emotions. Knowing how to help clients overcome addiction once and for all will be extremely helpful. Intuitively consider using the tools found in this chapter to help facilitate this.

Chapter 10: Addiction Recovery

Taking Full Responsibility

The first step to overcoming any addiction, of course, is being completely and totally honest about the struggles that you are facing. Unfortunately, rarely do people want to face or admit problems when they arise, so they often go untreated and get worse and worse.

When helping clients with addictions, have them write down and answer the following questions:
- The addiction that I have struggled with is . . .
- This is affecting me in the following ways . . .
- This is costing me . . .
- If things don't change . . .

Encourage them to be completely honest with themselves.

Awareness, when followed by a solution, is the first step to change. This leads us to the next step, which is making a firm *decision* to make changes in their life. You may tell your clients, "I can give you helpful tools until the cows come home, but if you haven't actually *decided* that things are going to be different from here on out, it isn't going to make much of a difference." After honesty comes the time to make a decision.

Have your clients take a moment and make a list of all of the ways that life will be different once they are completely free.
- How will that feel?
- What is your "why" for recovering?

Have your clients use these answers to help them get through the difficult moments of recovery and keep them motivated. Encourage your clients by sincerely saying, "Allow yourself to hope for a better future and to believe in your heart that change and full recovery is truly possible. I believe in you, and you get to believe in yourself as well."

The Mentor's Toolbox

Separating the Addiction from the Identity

Explain the following to your clients:

I want to make it extremely clear that YOU are not your addiction. I've heard way too many people introduce themselves and say, "I am an addict." I get that they are simply trying to come clean with what they are going through, but a critical part of recovery is removing your addiction from your identity. Think about that for a moment; most people who struggle with addictions identify with their addictions, and because it is so embedded in their minds at an identity level, they almost always relapse, even if they have a period of sobriety. Those who believe themselves to be smokers tend to smoke. Those that believe themselves to be alcoholics tend to drink. Those that believe themselves to be gamblers tend to gamble. They might go a number of months or even years without participating in those activities, but those who *identify* with their addictions almost always go back to them at some point or another.

I once heard a story of a frog who met a scorpion at the edge of a lake. The scorpion asks the frog if he would be willing to carry him across the lake, to which frog responds, "No way! I'm a frog, and you're a scorpion. If I help you, you'll sting me, and I'll die." The scorpion says, "Come on now, Mr. Frog. You are my only hope to get across the lake. Please help me." The frog says, "How do I know that you won't sting me along the way?" "Mr. Frog," the scorpion replies, "Think about it! I can't swim, so if I sting you, yes, you'll die, but I'll die too. It wouldn't make any sense for me to do so." The frog thinks about it and decides that the scorpion has a point, so he reluctantly consents, and the scorpion hops aboard the frog's back. Well, sure enough, about halfway across the lake, the scorpion stings the frog, and with his last breath, the frog proclaims, "What did you do that

Chapter 10: Addiction Recovery

for? You just stung and killed me, but you've also killed yourself. Why would you do that?" to which the scorpion responds, "Because I'm a scorpion, and that's what we do—we kill frogs!"

As ludicrous as this analogy sounds, its true for so many people. When we identify with certain things, we by nature tend to act certain ways. If you identify as an addict, chances are you are going to have addictive behaviors, so the very first step is to remove the addiction that you struggle with from your personal identity. Never, ever again say the words, "I am an addict." If you must talk about it, state your name and that you are recovering from an addiction. The first step is to be honest about the struggles that you are going through, but never to the point of identifying with the addiction itself.

Have your clients write down the following:

I struggle with addiction but I am NOT my addiction. I am a powerful, brilliant, beautiful child of the divine with limitless potential and the power to create anything and everything that I desire.

Now have your clients place their hand over their heart and declare out loud, "I am free!"

The Mentor's Toolbox

Identify the Root of the Addiction

Most addictions come from an attempt to numb or cover up what I like to refer to as "soul wounds" (more on that on page 130). On a piece of paper, draw a rough outline of a human body. It doesn't have to be a masterpiece, but make a depiction of a body. Most people have soul wounds in their bodies. We store emotions regarding different circumstances and different people in different areas of our body, and these stem from highly emotional experiences that took place during our growing-up years.

For example, let's say that you are four years old and you move houses. You are so excited because you finally have your own room. You are as excited as can be, and you like to draw and express your excitement artistically. So the very first night in your new room you realize that you have four brand-new white walls. So you take out your markers and go to town on these new white walls; you draw a picture of your mom, your dad, your brothers, your sisters, your dog, your best friend, and when you finish you take a moment to admire your work and then yell, "Daddy! Daddy! Come look at what I've done!" So your dad comes running into your room, and instead of seeing the excitement on your face, all he sees is that you've drawn all over the brand-new walls. He goes berserk and starts yelling at you. He takes your markers, throws them in the trash, then grabs your wrists and hits them with a ruler, causing you considerable pain. As a four-year-old, what did that experience lead you to believe? Maybe that feeling artistic and expressing yourself leads to pain? Maybe that your dad can't be trusted? Maybe that you aren't good enough? And without even realizing it you now have soul wounds in your wrists. While the physical wounds might only be temporary, emotional wounds can last a lifetime if we don't know how to help them heal.

Chapter 10: Addiction Recovery

Another example might be if a parent leaves you when you are really young either by choice or by passing on. This could lead to a feeling of abandonment, which is typically stored in the abdominal region of the body, which sometimes leads a person to use food to cover up or numb such emotions and gain weight. Extreme examples happen when a person goes through some sort of abuse. If a person experiences sexual abuse, for example, they will often form soul wounds in their gender areas. Soul wounds can sometimes form when a child is bullied or if they feel like they don't fit in. Each person needs to feel like they belong and can contribute in some way, so being consistently belittled or made to feel lonely because you do not feel accepted can lead to soul wounds.

People say that some addictions form out of an attempt to fit in, such as social smoking or social drinking. I would be so bold as to say that, while this is certainly a part of it, they are likely even more trying to numb the pain of how they would feel if they weren't accepted and didn't fit in. Soul wounds, especially when accompanied by addictive behaviors, often lead to shame.

There is a major difference between guilt and shame. Although it does not feel good, guilt is a very positive emotion. It informs us that we've done something wrong and motivates us to make changes. On the other hand, shame is the counterfeit of guilt. It causes a person to want to run and hide. Because most people feel shame because of their addictive behaviors, they will often turn back to the addictive behavior to numb the feelings of shame, which of course brings more shame and more addictive behavior. It is a very vicious cycle.

When you feel that this tool is appropriate, invite your clients to draw a rough outline of a body on a piece of paper. Then, tapping into intuition, invite them to make dots all over the body to mark all of the places that they feel they have soul wounds and to then mark where each one stems from, such as a specific incident or series of incidents that took place, as well as all of the negative emotions that they feel reside in each soul wound. Ask how each incident made them feel. Have them write down a list of all negative emotions underneath each soul wound. Finally, invite your clients to identify which one, or which ones, are the soul wounds that they use their addiction to numb or cover up. You have now identified the root of the addiction and may proceed with emotional clearing or breakthrough tools you feel would be most appropriate.

Chapter 10: Addiction Recovery

Swish Pattern

After identifying the root of the addiction and asking if it is OK with their unconscious mind to make a change today and for them to be aware of it consciously, use the following with your clients to replace the destructive behavior with a more desired behavior:

Our next step is to break the pattern that leads to the addictive behavior and replace it with a new one. We will be using a tool called a swish pattern, which will require you to create visual images in your mind.

Tap into intuition and ask yourself how you know it's time to participate in your addictive behavior. What is the trigger? For example, if your addictive behavior is gambling, it might be walking through a hotel or cruise ship that happens to have a casino and seeing the poker tables or the slot machines. If it's food, think about what happens right before you begin reaching for the food. Whatever it is, think about what it is that triggers the addictive behavior, and get a visual imagine of it in your mind. Good, now clear your mind.

What would you like to feel or do instead of participating in your addictive behavior? Create a picture of you doing this new behavior in your mind. Now, do so looking through your own eyes—see what you would see as if you were actually performing that new behavior. Good, now step out of the picture so that you see your body in the picture. Excellent, now clear your mind.

Now bring the old image back into your mind. Step into the picture so that you are looking at it through your own eyes and allow the image to fill the screen of your mind. Now take the image of the new behavior and put it in the lower left-hand corner of your mind, small and dark. When I say, "Whoosh!" bring up that picture and make it explode BIG and BRIGHT on the screen of your mind, while the old picture of your old behavior rapidly shrinks to a distant point and disappears. This can happen as quickly as 1, 2, 3—Whoosh! Are you ready? 1 . . . 2 . . . 3 . . . Whoosh!

Good, now open your eyes, and close your eyes once again. Good. We will do this faster and faster, starting with the image of your old behavior (which we will refer to as your present state) centered and the image of your new behavior (which we will refer to as the desired state) in the lower left-hand corner, small and dark.

When I say, "Whoosh," bring the desired state up and make it explode BIG and BRIGHT on the screen, while the present state picture rapidly shrinks to a distant point and disappears. This can happen as quickly as 1, 2, 3... Whoosh!

Are you ready? Present state, desired state, 1, 2, 3... Whoosh! Eyes open, eyes closed. Present state, desired state 1, 2, 3... Whoosh! Eyes open, eyes closed.

We are going to do this several times.

Present state, desired state 1, 2, 3 . . . Whoosh! Eyes open, eyes closed.
Present state, desired state 1, 2, 3 . . . Whoosh! Eyes open, eyes closed.
Present state, desired state 1, 2, 3 . . . Whoosh! Eyes open, eyes closed.
Present state, desired state 1, 2, 3 . . . Whoosh! Eyes open, eyes closed.
Present state, desired state 1, 2, 3 . . . Whoosh! Eyes open, eyes closed.
Present state, desired state 1, 2, 3 . . . Whoosh! Eyes open, eyes closed.
Present state, desired state 1, 2, 3 . . . Whoosh! Eyes open, eyes closed.
Present state, desired state 1, 2, 3 . . . Whoosh! Eyes open, great job!

Now think about what used to trigger the old behavior. What image do you have in mind now? If done correctly, it should automatically go to the new behavior. If it doesn't, do this exercise until you no longer think of your old behavior.

Now how do you feel about that old behavior? How is it different now? In your mind, project yourself into the future and see the old trigger which would have led you to participate in your former addic-

Chapter 10: Addiction Recovery

tive behavior, and what happens instead? If you still see yourself going back to the old behavior, repeat this process until you see yourself doing the new behavior. Once you see yourself futuristically doing the new behavior, congratulations! You have just created a new pattern in your mind.

The Mentor's Toolbox

CHAPTER 11
WEALTH CREATION

The tools found in this chapter are primarily used to assist your clients to improve their relationship with money and develop a more positive money mindset. All aspects of success come down to relationships. If your clients have a negative relationship with money, they will likely struggle to receive it in large quantities.

Because money tends to be such a sensitive subject, the tools in this chapter may seem hokey to your clients the first time you use them, and that's OK. I frequently repeat T. Harv Eker's motto, "I'd rather be really hokey and really rich than really cool and really broke. How about you?"

As with any mentoring tool, be mindful of your clients' needs. Some may have the misconception that, by incorporating these tools, you are somehow encouraging them to overly "love" or "worship" money. If this comes up, kindly remind your clients that money itself is neutral, neither good nor bad. Money is not the root of all evil. If it was, all of the spiritual, usually quite wealthy leaders found in spiritual texts would be going straight to hell. Money simply magnifies a person's inner intentions. The more money a person earns, the more people he or she can help and the greater their influence can be.

Chapter 11: Wealth Creation

Financial Thermostat

T. Harv Eker, author of *Secrets of the Millionaire Mind* and the genius whose teachings inspired the majority of the tools in this chapter, explains that it all begins with what he calls a person's *financial thermostat*. Think of a regular thermostat. If you walk into a room that is 72 degrees, it is pretty likely that the thermostat in that room is set at 72 degrees. You could open a door or window, allow some air to enter the room to raise or lower the temperature by a few degrees, but eventually that thermostat is going to kick on and drive that room right back to 72 degrees. It's the same when it comes to money.

How many lottery winners have you heard of that were just as broke a few years later as before they won? This is because, even though they amassed a large fortune, their financial thermostats were still set very low. Contrast that with a gentleman I'm sure you've heard of who goes by the name of Donald Trump. Trump is a multi-billionaire who has actually lost everything he had on multiple occasions. Since his financial thermostat was set for billions, each time he lost his money he made it all back and then some within a few short years.

How do you help your clients figure out where their thermostat is set? It's simple: invite them to take a look at their current financial results. If they are like millions of people who have been banging their heads against the wall trying to figure out why their financial situation is going nowhere, it is probably because their thermostat is not set for any higher than the amount of money they are currently receiving. If your clients' financial thermostat is not set for high levels of success, large amounts of money will probably never come to them. Thankfully, there is hope. Regardless of what their thermostat is set for, there are steps that you can take to help them change it.

As always, the first step when it comes to change is awareness. Eker explains that each person's financial thermostat is usually formed during childhood from three main elements:

What you heard about money:
If you grew up in a home that was anything like mine, you probably heard all of the clichés like "money doesn't grow on trees," "money can't buy happiness," "money is the root of all evil," etc. Let's use that last one as an example. If you are indoctrinated with the idea that having money will make you evil, what will you do, possibly without even realizing it, when you get money?

What you saw regarding money:
What was your parents' relationship with money like as you were growing up? Did they have a positive relationship or a negative relationship? Were your parents good at managing money or were they frivolous with it? Did you ever walk in on your parents arguing about money or complaining about having to pay bills? All of these affect our financial thermostat.

What you experienced with money:
A young nurse who went through one of Eker's programs wanted to figure out why her financial state was where it was. She made good money as a nurse but could never seem to hang on to it. She was completely broke at the end of each month and couldn't figure out what to do about it. She recalled having an experience when she was eight years old. Her parents took her out to a fancy Chinese restaurant, and when the bill for the meal came, her mother and father began a heated, bitter argument over money and the cost of the expensive meal. Her father, enraged, stood up to storm out of the restaurant, when he collapsed right there at the table from a heart

attack. At eight years old, this girl was on her community's swim team and jumped down to administer CPR to her father. He died right there in her arms. From that moment on, she subconsciously associated money with the feelings of pain and death, so she naturally got rid of money each time she received it.

Invite your clients to answer the following questions on a piece of paper:
1. What I heard about money growing up was . . .
2. What I saw regarding money growing up was . . .
3. What I experienced with money growing up was . . .

Once this is completed, utilize the tools you feel would be most appropriate from the Breakthrough chapter to help your clients reprogram how they view money. End with them doing the Morter March while thinking the words, "I am thankful and grateful that I now have unlimited finances. I am thankful and grateful that I now have unlimited finances. I am thankful and grateful that I now have unlimited finances."

Becoming Wealthy System

Regardless of what your clients' main goals are throughout their time working with you, a natural result of growing oneself can be to grow one's wealth. Money is attracted to order, therefore you must teach your clients to become excellent at managing their money. This does *not* mean using a budget. Please, encourage your clients to cut the word "budget" out of their vocabulary! It denotes lack and creates a glass ceiling over one's wealth as it basically states that there is a limited amount of income to be made, therefore even less money must be spent. I don't know about you, but I can't stand to even *think* that way! Managing one's money well does not mean restricting oneself to a scarcity mindset. In fact, it is quite the opposite. The following is a money management tool, based on T. Harv Eker's Jar System, that will help your clients become wealthy, should they choose to do so.

Invite your clients to go to their bank or credit union and open up several subaccounts under their name so that they have a total of six, including their checking account. Once the accounts have been set up, instruct your clients to name the accounts as follows:

- Essentials (this will be their normal checking account)
- Generosity
- Education
- Financial Freedom Fund
- Wealth Accumulation Account
- Celebration

Depending on your clients' bank or credit union, they may be able to rename and manage these accounts online. Instruct them, each time they get paid, to separate their after-taxes money as follows:

Chapter 11: Wealth Creation

50% of their earnings will go into their Essentials Account. This will be for their basic living expenses such as a mortgage, rent, groceries, utilities, car payments, gasoline, clothing, miscellaneous, debt repayment, etc.

10% of their earnings will be used specifically to give away. If they belong to a church that practices tithing, that will come from this, their Generosity Account. If they also give away an additional amount to help the poor (such as a fast offering), this will come out of their essentials account. If they are not a member of a church that practices tithing, invite your clients to simply give to a charity of their choice.

10% of their earnings will go towards furthering their education. This will be for registering for seminars, purchasing books and audio recordings, and hiring additional mentors. If they took out loans to participate in your mentoring program, the money in this account could go towards making the monthly payments. Each time your clients gain a new marketable skill, they become a little more valuable, and their potential for wealth creation goes up. Encourage them to be a lifelong learner and watch their incomes continue to rise.

10% of their earnings will go into their Financial Freedom Fund, which will be used specifically for making investments that will ultimately bring them passive income streams. This is their golden goose. It is never spent, only invested and then replaced. An example of an appropriate use for the funds in this account may be a down payment on what will be a rental property.

10% of their earnings will go into their Wealth Accumulation Account. This is used similar to a savings account. Instruct your clients that they will want to have some liquid savings, but some of the money in this account may be put into a more semi-liquid vehicle that will generate interest, such as whole life insurance.

Finally, 10% of their earnings will be used to celebrate their progress and their accomplishments. Most people believe that practice makes perfect, but this is a misconception. Practice makes *permanent.* This is why the advice to live like a pauper for the first seventy years of your life, eating rice and beans and living way below your means while stashing money away until you retire simply doesn't work. No one has ever scrimped their way to great wealth. Teach your clients that the money in their celebration account will be for practicing what it is like to be wealthy. Once a month, tell them to take themselves out for what I like to call an *abundance experience*. This may include going to a five-star restaurant. This may include staying at an amazing resort for an evening or spending a few hours at the most luxurious spa in town. They are practicing *feeling* wealthy so that they eventually *become* wealthy. What happens inside their brain is the building of *neuroassociations* (as discussed on page 127). Everything in your life is connected to one of two things: pain or pleasure. A reason why many fail to reach success is because they link the process of becoming successful with pain. The purpose of the celebration account is to link success with high amounts of pleasure. Encourage your clients to use this account each and every month. If they do not, they will be depriving themselves of incredible experiences and stunting their own progress. They may be tempted to use this money to pay off debt faster. Warn them to RESIST THIS TEMPTATION! The brain will not create additional financial results if one's sole purpose in doing so is paying off debt. Ask your clients what they would do if money was no object. Encourage your clients to use the money in their celebration account to enjoy their abundance experience guilt-free and truly begin to enjoy life!

If, for whatever reason, your clients choose not to use bank accounts for their becoming wealthy system, they can use jars or envelopes at home instead. This would make sense if they are cur-

Chapter 11: Wealth Creation

rently working in a position where their primary income is cash, such as waiting tables in a restaurant.

You may have clients whose current financial circumstances do not seem to allow them to live off of 50% of their income. What if your clients are barely scraping by financially? The *habit* in this case is much more important than the *amount.* This means if your clients need to start off with dividing $1 per month into six coins and putting them into six different jars, then that's what they do. Tell them to put the ten cents in their celebration jar, go to the store, buy a tiny piece of candy and enjoy the heck out of it! Then, the following month, they can divide $2 into their jars, then $4, then $8, and so on. Again, money is attracted to order, so the more your clients implement this system, the more money can come to them.

The Mentor's Toolbox

Money Personality Types

Just as everyone has a dominant personality color, everyone also has a dominant "money personality." As you work with clients who wish to increase their income, cash flow, and net worth, it will be important that you help them identify what their money personality type is and then teach them what part of the Becoming Wealthy System to specifically focus on to achieve their desired results. The four money personality types are Spender, Saver, Avoider, and Money Monk.

Spenders: These are the people who feel that money is "burning a hole in their pocket." They can't wait to get their next paycheck because that means they have more money to spend. Their favorite of the six accounts in the Becoming Wealthy System will be, of course, the Celebration Account. Encourage them, however, to focus their attention on the Wealth Accumulation Account. Setting aside 10% of their earnings may be a struggle for them at first, but it will be essential for their growth and success to create that balance for themselves.

Savers: These are the people that do not like spending money. They always believe they need to save money for a "rainy day" that never comes. Extreme cases are hoarders. They tend to live out of fear of "what if I need it?" so they rarely spend money on things that they enjoy and rarely are willing to invest in things. Their favorite account will be the Wealth Accumulation Account because it will be what they are used to. Encourage them to focus on the Celebration Account and the Financial Freedom Fund.

Avoiders: These are the people who hate money and anything to do with it. They would rather we not use money as a form of currency. They avoid looking at their bank accounts and generally procrastinate paying bills. They tend to get a lot of late charges and overdraft fees. Simply following the Becoming Wealthy System will be helpful to them.

Money Monks: There are some people that believe that money, somehow, makes them less spiritual. They may have deeply rooted beliefs that money is evil and should be avoided at all costs. They tend to live minimalistic lives and struggle receiving financial compensation for services they provide. While it may take some persuading, strongly encourage them to follow the Becoming Wealthy System. Help them understand that money isn't evil, nor does it make a person less spiritual. Take your time and be patient with money monks.

Debt vs. Loans

There is a huge difference between good debt and bad debt. Bad debt is an expense that takes money out of your pocket, such as consumer debt, education that you don't use, and so forth. Yes, education can very much fall under the category of bad debt if you don't use it to create a return on your investment. How many people do you know that have spent years in college pursuing a degree that they don't use? Now they have thousands and thousands of dollars that they must pay back for a piece of paper with their name on it hanging on the wall.

Good debt, or *loans*, means using someone else's money to put more money into your pocket. Education that you do use is a great example. For example, if you go to school to become an attorney and then take that education to create a very successful law practice, that education falls into the category of a loan, or good debt. For me, hiring personal mentors was a fantastic use of good debt. I borrowed tens of thousands of dollars from banks and credit unions to hire the best mentors I could find and then used what they taught me to create an enormous return on that investment over and over and over again. While many middle class people view debt like a crushing weight that they desperately want to remove, the wealthy use loans like a platform to get ahead financially.

Think of it this way. Let's say you make $2,000 a month, and that what you owe in credit card fees, personal loans, etc., is $10,000. Let's say that your monthly expenses are $1,500 per month, leaving you with $500 left over. What most middle class people tend to do is put the entire $500 towards paying down the $10,000. Think about that for a moment. If you were paying $500 towards a $10,000 debt, you would need to be paid twenty times to pay the entire amount off,

Chapter 11: Wealth Creation

not factoring in any interest. Now let's say you do what a lot of soon-to-be wealthy people do and pay only the minimum payment of $100 towards your loans for a certain period of time, leaving you with $400 to invest each month. Let's say you also take out a few extra loans to invest in assets, hire a personal mentor to teach you new skills, and that you start applying these new skills over a twelve-month period. You now owe $40,000 rather than $10,000, but you are now making $50,000 per month instead of only $2,000. Let's assume that your expenses are now $5,000 per month, leaving you with a $45,000 per month cash flow. Even though what you owe is now significantly higher, your income is also much higher and, in this case, you could pay off all of what you owe in a single month.

Obviously this is all hypothetical, but this is how successful people think. This is an extremely important concept to teach your clients. Help them understand that it is 100% OK to borrow money to purchase assets that earn them more money, including their greatest asset: their mind. If your clients want to be rich, they must think and act like rich people.

Chapter 11: Wealth Creation

The $50,000 Question

A person's money mindset can be determined with a single question: What would you do if I handed you $50,000 cash right now that was tax-free and no strings attached? A stereotypical poor-minded person will answer with all of the "stuff" that they would buy, including new cars, new toys, new vacations, or they might say that they would give most of it away. A stereotypical middle class-minded person will say that they would pay off debts before anything else. A stereotypical wealth-minded person would say that they would invest the money to purchase assets and then use the cash flow to use purchasing whatever else they would like.

Use this $50,000 question to help your clients determine what type of mindset they currently have, and help them see what further changes they will need to make to get to where they really want to be.

The Mentor's Toolbox

Thirty-Day Spending Exercise

Invite your clients to number a blank sheet of paper from one to thirty and to then imagine that each of those numbers represents a day in a month. They are to imagine that every day for thirty straight days they must spend $1,000. They must spend the entire amount, meaning they are not allowed to figuratively put some in a savings account or stash some money away for later.

This tool is especially helpful for those who grew up in households where extreme hoarding was taught. This tool is also useful to help identify a person's spending habits and what adjustments can be made. The money from the first several days will likely be used to pay bills, buy groceries, and pay down debt. The interesting part of the exercise comes when they no longer have any bills or debt that needs to be paid. What happens then? Do they spend the rest of the money buying junk? Do they get rid of the money as quickly as possible (this could help identify some more deeply rooted financial beliefs)? Do they use the money to invest in passive income strategies that will lead to financial freedom?

Chapter 11: Wealth Creation

Money Letters

To further improve your clients' relationship with money, you may encourage them to write letters to each of the men that are found on the various dollar bills. For easy reference, George Washington is found on the $1 bill, Thomas Jefferson is found on the $2 bill, Abraham Lincoln is found on the $5, Alexander Hamilton on the $10 bill, Andrew Jackson on the $20, Ulysses S. Grant on the $50 bill, and Benjamin Franklin on the $100 bill.

This exercise is enhanced when the clients look at the picture on the dollar bill that is being addressed. The letters start by addressing the person by his first name. This is done to further emphasize that money is a relationship. If your clients were writing to the $1 bill, they might write something such as,

"Dear George,

Thank you for being part of my life. I would greatly appreciate if you and all of your friends came to stay with me more often. What must I do to make this happen?

Love,
Eric"

Once this is completed, invite your clients to write a "response" from that particular dollar bill. Encourage them to write whatever comes to their mind, not worrying about whether or not it makes sense. Often they will write words of encouragement, counsel, and insight as to what they can do to improve their relationship with money. An example may be,

"Dear Eric,

I'm so glad to have received your letter today. I have been waiting to hear from you for quite some time. I would love to come and stay with you more often, and so would my other friends. We like you a lot. We haven't been over to your house very often because you need to find more ways to add value to the lives of others. We hang out at the houses of those who add the most value to others. You have many skills and special talents. Use them to bless as many lives as possible, and we will be there more often than you will know what to do. You are special and worthy. I can't wait to see you again soon.

Sincerely,
George"

Repeat this process with all the other people found on US currency, or with all of the people on the paper currency used in your clients' place of residence.

Chapter 11: Wealth Creation

Money Tantrum

If you can tell that your clients have a great deal of pent-up stress or other negative emotion surrounding money, you may encourage them to use this tool. Invite your clients to take a bundle of cash (even if it is a handful of $1 bills) in their hands and then throw a money tantrum. They might express frustration that they have never felt like there has been enough money to go around. They may say things like "You changed my best friend and turned him into a scumbag!" Encourage your clients to hold absolutely nothing back. They may throw the money onto the floor, stomp on it, whatever they need to do to let everything that they have on their chest go. This may last several minutes, and your clients may be exhausted once they have finished. Once they stop, ask if there is any more that needs to be expressed. If they say yes, invite them to keep going until the tank is completely empty, holding nothing back. If they say that they have expressed everything that they needed to say, it is now time to do the second half of this exercise, which is one of healing and bonding with money.

Invite your clients to gather all of the money up and hold it in their hands. Next, invite them to apologize to the money for holding onto all of the negative emotions. Encourage them to speak kind words to the money and invite it to come and stay with them more often since they promise to be much nicer from now on. Again, this tool is useful in helping your clients release large amounts of pent-up negative emotion towards money.

Money Bonfire

This is a tool to use if you sense that your clients have an unhealthy attachment to money which is creating scarcity. Carefully build a fire; this could be on an outside grill, in an indoor fireplace, or simply have a lighter ready to go. Tell your clients that they will need to bring a $100 bill for this exercise. Once the flame is big enough, inform your clients that in just a moment, when you say, "1, 2, 3—now!" they are going to toss the $100 bill into the fire but not to do so until they are specifically instructed to do so. Invite them to approach the fire and get ready to burn the money. "On the count of 3. 1 . . . 2 . . . STOP! STOP! STOP!" You want your clients to get as close as possible to burning the money without actually doing so. The purpose of this exercise is to stir up emotion regarding money without actually destroying it. Once you say "STOP!" invite your clients to journal on everything that is going through their mind and all the emotions that they can feel. Consider using this in conjunction with the Belief Breakthrough exercise found on page 120. Note that if you are not in a place where it would be safe to use actual fire, you may instruct your clients to tear the $100 bill up instead of burning it. Again, get them to think that they are about to destroy the money without actually doing so.

Chapter 11: Wealth Creation

$100 Bill in the Wallet

The sad truth is that many of the people that you will work with will struggle with money. Some will come to you with such a negative relationship with money that even the concept of having some will be enough to trigger them. This is a tool to help them begin to improve their relationship with money because it uses real, tangible cash. Invite your clients to carry in their wallet or purse a $100 bill at all times. Every time they open their wallet or purse, they will see it and remember that they have money.

Remember that a major part of what you do as a mentor is to uncover limiting beliefs and negative emotion that your clients have inside of them so that they can be cleared and replaced with positive beliefs and emotions. This tool may uncover fears of loss that your clients have. They may share with you that they are worried that the money may get stolen. Help your clients work through these fears and use the emotional release and breakthrough tools in this book when appropriate.

If your clients don't have $100, invite them to start small and gradually work their way up to having $100. Start with a $1 bill, then graduate to a $2 bill (most banks carry them), then a $5 bill, and so on until they have a $100 bill that they keep with them at all times.

$100 Bill on the Mirror

This is a tool that you can use with your clients to help them associate earning money with receiving inspiration. Invite them to tape a $100 bill to the top right corner of their bathroom mirror where they will be able to see it every day as they get ready in the morning and as they prepare to go to bed. This will cause them to look up and to the right to see the money, activating the same portion of the brain that is activated when looking for inspiration regarding a future event. As they do this exercise day after day, they may notice that ideas come to their mind. Encourage your clients to immediately write these ideas down and then put them into action. They may be surprised that, by doing so, more money comes into their lives.

Just like the "$100 bill in the wallet" tool, your clients may start with a $1 bill and gradually work themselves up to a $100 bill.

Chapter 11: Wealth Creation

$1 Million Bill

I'll never forget the feeling I had when I realized I had made my first million dollars. Just a few short years earlier, I had been on welfare and had purchased a chocolate bar in the shape of a $1 million bill from the dollar store. I ate every morsel of it imagining what it would be like to make $1 million. Fast forward a very short period and I had done it!

If your clients are planning on increasing their income over the next year, they will need to begin to visualize themselves with lots of money. One of the fastest ways to do this is to get a package of $1 million bills. These can be purchased online and sent to their home. Have your clients tape a million-dollar bill above their bathroom mirror, so that they see it every day as they are getting ready. Instruct them to keep two million-dollar bills inside their wallet so that, every time they open it, they see the money, and their mind receives a message that they are a multi-millionaire.

The Mentor's Toolbox

CALL TO ACTION

I want to personally thank you for purchasing and reading my book. I hope you have found it useful and will continue to use the tools found within its pages to change your own life and the lives of those whom you mentor and coach. Because you read this book, I want to offer you a special "thank you" gift worth over $2,500.00. In order to get the most out of this book, I am offering you two tickets to our next three-day Master Creator event, live in Salt Lake City, Utah, so that you and a guest may see the tools found in this book in action and experience them for yourself. (More information about this seminar, including when the next one will be held, can be found at http://FeelWellLiveWell.com/master-creator/.) Tickets are usually $1,297.00 each, but if you will commit to being there for the entire three days and playing full-on as if you had paid full price, you and a guest may register for the next class at *no* charge. To claim your free tickets, go to http://FeelWellLiveWell.com/master-creator/, click Register Now, enter your information, and use the promo code: scholarship (make sure it is all lower case letters and that there is no space after the word or it will say "invalid promo code") to make your price zero dollars. For assistance, email ClientServices@FeelWellLiveWell.com and let my team know that you have read this book and would like to attend our upcoming Master Creator event. Include a phone number to reach you, and someone will be in touch to help you claim your free tickets.

Do you want to take your mentoring/coaching business to the next level? Join us at our next event and inquire about our Successful

Mentor program. Over 80% of Successful Mentor graduates have earned $100,000 or more their very first full calendar year after graduating from the program. Want more information about The Successful Mentor program? Send me an email personally to Eric@FeelWellLiveWell.com with the subject heading "Info About The Successful Mentor." Please include a phone number to reach you, and I will make sure someone contacts you to give you all the details. Let's help you take your mentoring/coaching business to the next level so that you can reach all the lives you are meant to reach!

ACKNOWLEDGMENTS

A major thank you to Heather Bailey, Jack Canfield, T. Harv Eker, Tad James, Thomas Tadlock, Garrett Gunderson, Ron Williams, Greg O'Gallagher, Irina Baxter, Dr. M.T. Morter, Jr., Brendon Burchard, Tony Robbins, Kris Krohn, Gerald Rogers, Sharon Lechter, Napoleon Hill, Kirk Duncan, Ann Webb, Gary Chapman, Dr. Taylor Hartman, Noah St. John, and many more for the inspiration and creation of many of the tools found in this book. You truly are pioneers in the industry and are changing lives all over the world.

The Mentor's Toolbox

ABOUT THE AUTHOR

Eric Bailey is a professional mentor, trainer, and advanced holistic healthcare practitioner. Over the years, he has closely observed the habits of highly successful people. Implementing what he has learned, he has seen massive growth in his healthcare practice, health, and relationships, especially with his beautiful wife, Heather, and four beautiful children.

In one year alone, he grew his monthly income more than a hundredfold, going from welfare to wealthy and becoming a millionaire by age 30. He now seeks to share his secrets to success, which absolutely anyone can use. Eric is a powerful motivational speaker and has impacted the lives of thousands of people through his books, audio training CDs, seminars, personal mentoring programs, and healthcare practice in northern Utah.

His greatest desire is to improve the lives of millions of people around the globe by helping them achieve vibrant health, massive wealth, and successful, loving relationships.

www.ingramcontent.com/pod-product-compliance
Lightning Source LLC
Chambersburg PA
CBHW070544010526
44118CB00012B/1219